DO
THE
RIGHT
THING

DO
THE
RIGHT
THING

How Dedicated Employees Create Loyal Customers and Large Profits

JAMES F. PARKER

Vice President, Publisher: Tim Moore
Associate Publisher and Director of Marketing: Amy Neidlinger
Wharton Editor: Yoram (Jerry) Wind
Acquisitions Editor: Jennifer Simon
Editorial Assistant: Pamela Boland
Development Editor: Russ Hall
Digital Marketing Manager: Julie Phifer
Marketing Coordinator: Megan Colvin
Cover Designer: The Ingredient
Managing Editor: Gina Kanouse
Project Editor: Anne Goebel
Copy Editor: Krista Hansing Editorial Services, Inc.
Proofreader: Water Crest Publishing, Inc.
Senior Indexer: Cheryl Lenser
Compositor: Nonie Ratcliff
Manufacturing Buyer: Dan Uhrig

Wharton School Publishing offers excellent discounts on this book when ordered in quantity for bulk purchases or special sales. For more information, please contact U.S. Corporate and Government Sales, 1-800-382-3419, corpsales@pearsontechgroup.com. For sales outside the U.S., please contact International Sales at international@pearsoned.com.

Printed in the United States of America

Third Printing April 2008

ISBN-13: 978-0-13-234334-3
ISBN-10: 0-13-234334-7

Pearson Education LTD.
Pearson Education Australia PTY, Limited.
Pearson Education Singapore, Pte. Ltd.
Pearson Education North Asia, Ltd.
Pearson Education Canada, Ltd.
Pearson Educatión de Mexico, S.A. de C.V.
Pearson Education—Japan
Pearson Education Malaysia, Pte. Ltd.

Library of Congress Cataloging-in-Publication Data

Parker, James F. (James Francis), 1947-

   Do the right thing : how dedicated employees create loyal customers and large profits / James F. Parker.
      p. cm.
   ISBN-13: 978-0-13-234334-3 (hardback : alk. paper) 1. Southwest Airlines Co.—Management. 2. Airlines—United States—Management 3. Customer relations—United States. 4. Customer services—United States. I. Title.
   HE9803.S68P37 2008
   387.7068'3—dc22
                                 2007018393

To my mom, who taught me, "You'll catch more flies with honey than with vinegar."

And to my dad, who sat outside on the steps with the black soldiers who were not allowed to eat at the inside lunch counter during the long bus ride home to Texas after World War II.

Thanks for teaching me to do the right thing.

Contents

Acknowledgments

When people ask me what I am doing these days, since I retired as CEO of Southwest Airlines, I like to tell them that I am trying to avoid work, and it is a full-time job. I guess writing a book should qualify as work, but thanks to the outstanding publishing team at Pearson Education, it was a labor of joy.

I want to express my sincere appreciation to Senior Editor Jennifer Simon for her role in shepherding this first time author through the labyrinthine process of turning thoughts and stories into a book, to Development Editor Russ Hall for helping me find my own voice as an author, to Associate Publisher Amy Neidlinger for her insightful suggestions, and to Anne Goebel and Krista Hansing for their prompt and beneficial refinements of the manuscript. Special thanks go to Publisher Tim Moore, for believing that I had something worthwhile to say, and to author Barry Rosenberg, who initially suggested that I might have a book in me.

The book would not have been possible without the assistance of my longtime executive assistant, Marilyn Strickland, who understands the marvels of modern technology better than I ever will. Thanks for the weekends and evenings you spent on this project, Marilyn. Thanks also to the two good friends who reviewed the manuscript and shared their insights and comments.

Of course, I must also thank the people of Southwest Airlines, who started with a dream and turned it into an airline that changed the world. Thanks for being my inspiration, and for allowing me to be part of your team for 25 wonderful years.

My greatest debt of gratitude goes to my wife and friend, Pat. Thank you for your patience, love, and strength—and for our two wonderful children, James and Jennifer.

About the Author

James Parker is a lawyer by trade, having received both his undergraduate and law degrees from The University of Texas. After serving as law clerk to a federal judge and as an assistant attorney general of Texas, Jim joined the San Antonio law firm of Oppenheimer, Rosenberg, Kelleher, and Wheatley. As luck would have it, one of the cofounders of that law firm, Herb Kelleher, also cofounded a small Texas airline called Southwest, and Jim soon stumbled into the airline industry. After serving as outside counsel for Southwest for 7 years, Jim became General Counsel for 15 years and ultimately served as Southwest Airlines' CEO for 3 years, including the period of the 9/11 terrorist attack and its aftermath.

During Jim's tenure as CEO, Southwest was the only major airline to remain profitable after 9/11. It also became the largest domestic airline in the United States in terms of passenger enplanements, and its market capitalization (the value of its outstanding stock) exceeded that of all other U.S. airlines combined. Southwest was named as the most admired airline and one of the three most admired companies in America by *Fortune* magazine, Airline of the Year by *Air Transport World* magazine, and one of the World's Most Socially Responsible Companies by *Global Finance* magazine. Jim was also named co-CEO of the Year in 2001 by

Morningstar.com and was named to Institutional Investor's list of Best CEOs in America in 2004.

Jim's proudest accomplishment, however, comes from the fact that Southwest Airlines was able to protect the jobs of all of its employees, with no furloughs or pay cuts in the aftermath of 9/11, while also remaining profitable every year and, in fact, every quarter during his tenure as CEO. Jim is presently retired from the airline industry and serves on the board of directors of the successful Texas Roadhouse restaurant company. He also serves on the Advisory Council for the MIT Leadership Center. This is his first book.

Introduction

Most people have a passion for success and creative self expression somewhere deep inside them. They want to be part of something meaningful, to make a contribution, and to find fulfillment in what they do. Sadly, these yearnings are often managed out of people in the unrelenting quest for predictable mediocrity that most organizations pursue. People are seldom encouraged to be themselves, have fun, or seek fulfillment in their jobs. Instead, they are pushed to just do their jobs, meet their quotas, and not make waves. Think outside the box? Proceed at your own peril.

A lot of companies say their employees are their most important asset, but they don't really mean it. The truth is, they treat employees as depreciable assets, to be used up and then discarded. This is the root cause of the culture of conflict that infects many major corporations today.

You can see the results in any customer service business. When you ask for help at the drug store or hardware store, does the person you ask groan because you interrupted his other duties, or does he cheerfully walk you over to the proper aisle and start telling you about the products you could choose? When the cable guy shows up at your house, does he really care about your business, or does he spend most of his time telling you how lousy the cable company is and that you ought to get satellite?

The truth is that employees who love their jobs will cause customers to love their company. Employees who hate their jobs will make customers hate the company. Quite simply, people who enjoy their work do a better job than people who don't. And it doesn't necessarily relate to how much they are paid. From the shop floor to the executive suite, it can fairly be said that the most highly paid people in their professions often do the worst jobs.

The ultimate success of any organization requires consistently excellent performance at every level. Vibrant and successful organizations are not built on a feeling of detachment by employees. Rather, they are built on a culture of engagement, in which employees believe in the mission they are trying to accomplish and know that they are contributing to its success. People who are given the room to succeed usually will.

For 25 years, I had the opportunity to be associated with such a vibrant and successful organization, as outside counsel, then as General Counsel, and finally for three years as CEO of Southwest Airlines. To be sure, I was always thrilled to accept the many honors that were bestowed on our company—Airline of the Year, one of the three most admired companies in America, co-CEO of the year, one of the world's most socially responsible companies, and so forth. But I never deluded myself into thinking that I had much to do with it. I knew the honors really belonged to our people, who showed their dedication and spirit every day. In fact, in our written communications at Southwest Airlines, we always capitalized the *E* in *Employees*, the *C* in *Customers*, and the *S* in *Shareholders*, to help us remember why we were in business. As the guardian of our corporate culture, President Colleen Barrett was certain to correct anybody who did not show the proper respect for any of these three constituencies in their writing or otherwise.

To those who are looking for a definitive history of Southwest Airlines; or a critical commentary on the brilliant leadership of the company's legendary cofounder, Herb Kelleher; or what the airline's business strategy should be from here, this is not your book. Of course, no book that touches on Southwest Airlines can avoid some of the rich stories from its colorful past, or some mention of Herb, but this book is not really about Southwest Airlines. Rather, it is about some of the lessons I learned from working with the people of Southwest Airlines for more than 25 years—mostly frontline workers and employees, whose deeds truly defined the culture for which Southwest Airlines became famous.

The overriding lesson I learned doesn't involve a lot of management guru buzzwords and acronyms. It is the simplest of principles, which we learned from childhood: When in doubt, just do the right thing. It is still a pretty good rule for doing business, dealing with people, and building successful organizations.

Chapter 1

Stumbling into the Business World

Shortly after the public announcement that I would become Southwest Airlines' new CEO in June of 2001, I was on one of our planes, flying from San Antonio to Dallas. Once we were in the air and the flight attendants had finished serving their first round of refreshments (yes, you can expect more than one round on Southwest, even on a 55-minute flight), each of the flight attendants stopped by my seat to chat for a moment and wish me well.

The fellow next to me, who looked like a West Texas cowboy, took note of the flight attendants' comments. After the flight attendants resumed serving and bonding with other customers, the cowboy looked up from his newspaper and asked why the flight attendants all seemed to know me so well.

"Oh, I work at Southwest," I said. "We're just kind of like family."

"I figured that out," he said. "What do you do there?"

"Well, I've been the General Counsel for 15 years, but I just got a promotion."

Now the cowboy curiously looked me over. "You're that guy whose picture was in the paper."

"Yeah, I'm afraid it was in so many papers that my son and daughter want to know if they'll ever be able to pick up a newspaper without seeing a story about their father in it."

As I chatted with the cowboy, he filled me in on some of his experiences flying Southwest Airlines. It turned out that he was actually a lawyer from Amarillo who had been flying Southwest for all of the years it had been serving that city. He told me how Southwest had revolutionized his law practice. Suddenly, Amarillo was no longer just an isolated energy and farming town in the Texas Panhandle. He could practice law anywhere in Texas now. He could appear in court in Dallas in the morning, meet a client for lunch in Houston, and attend a State Bar function in Austin in the afternoon—and still get home to sleep in his own bed that night. Besides, he said, flying Southwest was fun. The flights were usually on time, the service was great, the planes were clean, and, best of all, the employees always seemed happy and cheerful. He hated it when he had to fly someplace Southwest didn't go.

Needless to say, this was all music to my ears, and I took in every word of it. The flight seemed all too short as we made a typical Southwest landing (touch the ground, hit the brakes, push up the thrust reverser, and get to the gate early). As the passengers stepped into the aisle and began to gather their belongings, the cowboy reached into the overhead bin and pulled out his Stetson. He turned to me with a look reflecting an intention to give me some serious advice, and he did.

"You've got a hell of a good airline here," he said. "Don't screw it up."

It was a fair comment. As Southwest won customer satisfaction awards time after time, while making consistent profits, researchers and competitors wondered how we did it. People had fun working at Southwest yet worked as hard and efficiently as any group of employees anywhere. Customers loved the airline, and shareholders appreciated the consistent profits. It's like the company had some "secret sauce" that no other company possessed.

Perhaps there is a grain of truth there. While it may be no secret, there are elements of corporate culture I believe in that are less than obvious. There is no hard formula or mystic process, but there is an honest, no-nonsense way of encouraging leadership up and down the ranks, of respecting each other and sharing human interests, and of hiring and nurturing that leads to a kind of corporate DNA many businesses would like to possess. There is no single pat (or secret) answer, but I'll be glad to share some of the aspects with you.

As a matter of fact, I'll try to tell you the whole darn story, so you might as well grab your favorite refreshment and settle in. As you will see, refreshments do play a role in the history of Southwest Airlines. In fact, legend has it that the idea for Southwest was hatched on a cocktail napkin. Our story will show that there is often some serendipity and good fortune to the way certain people handle a crisis or adversity, and some folks manage to do it with a smile. While there is no single formula for success, the goal of this book is to share a few experiences that might be useful, or at least interesting, for people at all levels of any organization.

So here goes. Everything I'm about to tell you is pretty much true.

Chapter 2

9/11

September 11, 2001, was one of the darkest days in America's history. It was also the beginning of the most traumatic and tumultuous period in the history of the airline industry. As we mourned for those who lost their lives in the horrific terrorist attacks of that day, we looked forward to the future with nervous apprehension.

Giving America the freedom to fly was no longer just an advertising slogan. It was now potentially life threatening, and it was certainly a company risking endeavor. Nobody knew for sure whether the free world would even have an airline industry after terrorists learned to use commercial airliners as guided missiles. In a world that had come to take mobility for granted, would we be forced to revert to locomotives and steamships for the movement of goods and people? Would the airline industry survive? Would our company survive? Nobody knew for sure.

In 98 short years since the Wright brothers' first sustained controlled flight, airplane travel had gone from a novelty to a way of life by 2001. For thousands of years, humans had dreamed of flying like the birds. Some of the greatest minds in history tried, and failed, to unlock the secrets of flight. After centuries of failed attempts, it took two obscure brothers from Ohio to achieve what many had come to fear was impossible. At long last, man could fly.

In reality, the Wright brothers' greatest invention probably was not the airplane, but rather the modern instrumented wind tunnel. With their wind tunnel, Wilbur and Orville were able to understand the subtleties of flight. Their wind tunnel allowed them to learn that previously accepted theories about the coefficient of flight were wrong and that they needed a new wing design. The wind tunnel allowed them to develop a propeller that wouldn't tear the wing apart. On December 17, 1903, the lessons learned from their wind tunnel experiments allowed Orville to stay aloft for 12 history changing seconds.

Knowledge gained from the Wright brothers' momentous breakthrough allowed aviation technology to advance with incredible speed through the twentieth century. The development of the jet engine in the middle of the century once again revolutionized flight. With the advent of the jet engine, nonstop flights in large airplanes could be accomplished at incredible speed. The jet engine not only made travel faster, it also made it a lot less expensive. From the introduction of the first passenger jet airplane in 1958, air travel steadily became more popular, and people were flying in ever increasing numbers. With the deregulation of the U.S.

airline industry in 1978, flying finally became affordable for the masses.

By 2001, airline travel had become part of the fabric of society throughout the industrialized world, and especially in the United States. Nationwide, the price of flying, when adjusted for inflation, was less than half what it had been in the 1960s. People depended on air travel for the conduct of their daily lives. Families took vacations, college students flew home on weekends, and some people even commuted to work on an airplane every day. Businesspeople depended on air travel for the conduct of their daily business affairs. Much of the flow of commerce and ideas throughout the world depended on air travel. Everybody simply accepted this marvel of twentieth century technology as a given.

The manifest impact of the airplane on modern society was never more dramatically demonstrated than during the three days following the terrorist attacks of September 11, 2001, when the skies were silent. No living American will ever forget the horror of watching United Airlines Flight 175 crashing into the South Tower of the World Trade Center, instantly vaporizing everybody on board. Suddenly, the world faced the chilling realization that another airplane, which had flown into the North Tower of the World Trade Center a few minutes earlier, had not done so by accident. Nor had it been an errant pilot flying a small private plane. It was American Airlines Flight 11.

As fragmentary reports came in, it seemed that another plane had crashed into the Pentagon building in Washington. It became clear that the free world was under attack. The world seemed to be in chaos as reports surfaced that yet another airplane was missing. United Flight 93 was last located somewhere over Pennsylvania. It was not headed toward its intended destination of San Francisco, but rather toward the nation's capitol in Washington, D.C.

Americans simply could not understand what was happening. Clearly, America was under attack, but by whom, and why? The Iron Curtain had fallen a decade earlier. Who could hate us enough to commit such mindless and vicious acts of mass murder? Everything seemed out of control. Should we launch a nuclear response? And if so, against whom? Would the entire planet soon be reduced to a glowing ember?

My first knowledge that an airplane had flown into the World Trade Center came as I listened to the radio news while driving to work. I called my executive assistant, Marilyn, who arrived at work early every morning. I told her something strange was happening and suggested she turn on CNN. She could fill me in when I got into the office.

When I arrived, Marilyn quickly filled me in on what CNN was saying, and I headed straight to the office of our president and chief operating officer, Colleen Barrett. At this point, we had no idea of the magnitude of the crisis we were facing. I arrived in Colleen's office simultaneously with members of our Dispatch and Customer Relations departments, who came bearing news. Dispatch had been in contact with the Federal Aviation Administration's control center. It appeared that the airplanes that had flown into the World Trade Center were not small private planes, but were, indeed, large commercial jet aircraft. Information was still sketchy. The FAA either did not know or was not saying at that point whose airplanes they were. We didn't think any of the planes were ours, but we had not yet established contact with all of our airborne flights. Airplanes routinely fly through areas where they are out of range for radio contact. We believed that was where our unaccounted for airplanes were, but we all held our breath.

The FAA quickly declared a state of extreme emergency and ordered every commercial and private airplane in the air to land *immediately.* The airplanes' planned destinations or routes did not matter. If there was a strip of concrete beneath them, they were to get on it immediately. Reports were coming in of additional aircraft that were making mysterious maneuvers, including one with which contact had been lost over Pennsylvania. Nobody knew how many teams of hijackers might be in the air. It was essential that all airborne craft get on the ground immediately.

Of course, we instantaneously activated our crisis center. Within a few minutes, a member our Dispatch department arrived to let us know that we had established contact with all of our planes, and they had all been instructed to land wherever they were. Everybody exhaled for the first time in about five minutes. We still had no assurance that our flights were free of hijackers, but at least we knew that none of our airplanes, flight crews, or customers had been lost at the World Trade Center or the Pentagon.

I don't know how many minutes passed before we received word that all of our flights were safely on the ground, but it seemed like an eternity. Finally, the word came. And boy, were we relieved when word came that all of our flights had landed safely—despite the fact that we had crew members, customers, and airplanes scattered across the country, where they did not expect or want to be. With that news, we all shed a tear of relief and said a prayer for the people trapped in the World Trade Center, in the Pentagon, and on the hijacked airplanes. Like aviation professionals all over the world, we shared the grief of our friends and colleagues at United and American Airlines, who had suffered so tragically.

September 11, 2001, was one of those history-changing days that will be remembered forever by freedom loving Americans. The impact of that day on the American psyche is difficult to convey. To Britons, who saw their majestic capital city bombed nightly during World War II, the idea of a foreign attack might not seem so unimaginable. To the French, the Czechs, or the Poles, who have seen their countries ruthlessly occupied in the last century, violent attacks on freedom might not seem so incredible. To Germans who witnessed the horrific fire bombing of Dresden, the sorrowful melancholy felt by Americans as they watched the towers of the World Trade Center crumble into a terrible mass of death and debris would not have been unprecedented. To Japanese who had seen two cities destroyed by atomic bombs, the magnitude of the attack on the World Trade Center might not have been so shocking.

But Americans had nothing to which to compare this unprovoked attack on their land. Americans had saved the world from tyranny in two World Wars, but the battles had always been fought somewhere else. Not since the War of 1812 had there been a foreign attack on American soil in North America. Americans were justifiably outraged. And we were understandably frightened.

We all knew that what had happened was not an attack on United or American Airlines. It was an attack on America and on the entire free world. It was an attack on our freedom. The terrorists didn't just want to kill the people in the World Trade Center, the Pentagon, and whatever destination was saved through the heroism of the passengers on United Flight 93. The hijackers wanted to terrorize us and make us afraid. They wanted to destroy our way of life and take away our freedom. Now the whole world would have to fight for its freedom to fly, and we were all in the struggle together.

Chapter 3

The Question Was Answered...

The first business decision we faced on September 11, 2001, was what to tell our customers who would be calling to cancel their flight reservations. As horrifying as the 9/11 attack was for all Americans, it was certain to have a monumental impact on their attitudes toward flying.

From experience, we knew that almost any unsettling news would cause some nervous flyers to change their plans. An airplane crash anywhere in the world would have a significant effect. The first Gulf War in 1990 had a tremendous effect, ultimately leading to the bankruptcy of several airlines. The vision of an airplane crashing into the World Trade Center on worldwide television was certain to have an unprecedented effect. We knew that the calls would start coming immediately.

The airline industry is something of a cash flow business. Most airline tickets that are sold today are advance purchase, nonrefundable tickets. In other words, at any given time, an airline may be holding hundreds of millions of dollars that customers have paid for flights that will not take place for days, weeks, or months. Airlines depend on this continuous flow of unearned cash to pay their bills and meet their payrolls. If an airline suddenly had to give all of this cash back, it could quickly drain the coffers.

We did not have time to do an economic analysis. Even before we had established contact with all of our flights, the Customer Relations and Reservations agents had to know what to tell customers who would want to cancel their flights and get a refund. When I walked into the office of our president, Colleen Barrett, on the morning of 9/11, it was clear that we had to make an instantaneous decision. The head of our Customer Relations department, Jim Ruppel, arrived almost simultaneously. He knew the calls would be coming. Colleen's first instinct was the same as mine, as I knew it would be.

In the absence of any real information, we simply decided to follow our gut and do what we perceived to be the right thing. We decided that any customer who asked for a refund could have it, no questions asked, with no penalties or refund fees. To be honest, we probably did not fully appreciate the risk involved in this decision. At this point, the full magnitude of the terrorist attacks had not become clear. We really just knew that two planes had flown into the World Trade Center, and we knew that refund requests typically came after any aviation accident, or almost any unsettling world event. We certainly did not know that we would be unable to operate a single flight for three days, or that we would be unable to resume a normal schedule for six days. Nor did we know that, even after flights resumed, the level of passenger demand would drop so precipitously that it would not return to pre–9/11 levels for at least three years. In the absence of this knowledge, we simply did what we thought was the right thing to do.

As soon as we had a chance to catch our breath, we began to understand the magnitude of the crisis our industry faced. The skies were eerily silent. There was no way of knowing when we would be able to fly again, or whether anybody would be willing to get on an airplane. We knew we would need cash to survive, and, like every other airline, we quickly drew down our entire $500 million line of credit. A line of credit is basically a prearranged loan, whereby a bank or group of banks agrees to loan a business a certain amount of money upon request. Quite frankly, I was suspicious that some banks would renege on their obligations. There was already talk that some airlines would run out of money before they could resume flying. At least one, Midway Airlines, announced on September 12 that it would go out of business rather than try to resume operations. To their credit, however, the banks all honored their obligations. From that day forward, we monitored our cash balance on a daily basis, knowing that in this new world, cash would be king as never before.

The year 2000 had marked Southwest Airlines' twenty-eighth consecutive year of profitability. Every year since the company made its first profit in 1973, the airline had shared its profits with employees. Based on a formula we used, the portion of our 2000 profits to be paid into our employees' profit-sharing plan was $179.8 million, and it was due to be paid on September 14, 2001. Our cash balance going into September 11 was certainly adequate to meet all of our anticipated and reasonably unanticipated obligations, including our profit-sharing payment. Obviously, we did not anticipate a terrorist attack that would shut down our operations for an indeterminate period of time.

September 14 also turned out to be the day on which the Federal Aviation Administration allowed a limited resumption of flying activity. To be sure, we could not operate anything like a normal schedule. An airline is an intricate mélange of many moving parts—and all of our parts were out of place. We had airplanes, pilots, flight attendants, and even customers scattered all over the country, where they were not supposed to be. Flight crews had stayed with their airplanes, away from their families, so that they could fly the planes out whenever flying was permitted again. Where possible, we chartered buses to get passengers to their intended destinations. Some people rented cars and drove. In some cases, we simply had to rent hotel rooms and rely on our flight crews to care for and entertain our stranded customers. Some took their stranded passengers to movies. One crew, which was marooned in a city where we did not fly, took their passengers bowling. The pilots and flight attendants just pulled out their credit cards and did what was necessary to care for their passengers.

I shall never forget watching our first flight after September 11 take off from Dallas Love Field. All of our employees continued to come to work every day after 9/11, even though there were no flights, no bags, and no passengers. An aircraft normally buzzes with activity, and the air is filled with the sound of powerful jet engines magically lifting 50 tons of aluminum and precious human cargo into the air. For three days the airport had been silent. Business meetings and vacations had been canceled because people could not fly. Pallets of freight sat silently in the freight house. Mounds of mail awaited passage. And employees at every airline in America, including Southwest, worried that they might soon have no jobs.

When the FAA finally determined that flights could resume, under enhanced safety procedures, employees came pouring out of our headquarters building, training centers, maintenance base, and the airport itself to watch our first flight taxi to the end of the runway. Tears streamed down our cheeks as we heard the engines power up and begin the takeoff roll. People were waving American flags. Some spontaneously began singing *America the Beautiful*. The half dozen passengers on the plane could not hear the singing, but they could see the hundreds of employees lining the chain link fence next to the runway. Along with the employees, they felt the emotion of the moment. They knew that together we were fighting back. They knew we were once again exercising our freedom to fly. There was a sense of defiance and accomplishment in the moment as we watched the nose of our beautiful 737 lift into the sky.

Of course, there was still one small problem. We could give Americans the freedom to fly, but would they be *willing* to fly? It did not take long to see that passenger demand had dropped dramatically in the aftermath of the terrorist attacks. Some people were afraid to fly. Some businesses forbade flying by their executives, and almost everybody cut their travel budgets dramatically.

Even when we got all of our flight crews and airplanes back in position to fly a normal schedule, passengers were hard to find.

Every airline faced the same problem, and each had to decide how to respond. We all knew that passengers would be hard to come by. Almost in unison, all of the other major airlines announced that they were reducing their flying capacity by 20 percent, grounding 20 percent of their airplanes, and furloughing at least 20 percent of their employees. As they furloughed employees, several of those airlines invoked the so-called *force majeure* doctrine to avoid paying severance benefits. Tens of thousands of airline industry families suddenly found themselves with no jobs, no paychecks, and no severance pay to soften the transition.

At Southwest, we made a different decision. With the full support of our board of directors and the leadership of the chairman of our board, Herb Kelleher, we decided that Southwest would not lay off employees. We would not ground any of our airplanes. We would not cut the pay of our employees. And we would pay the $179.8 million to our employees' profit-sharing plan on time, on September 14, the same day our planes were allowed to return to the skies.

The only people who took a pay cut at Southwest Airlines were the company's officers, who we allowed to take a voluntary 10 percent pay reduction if they chose. (Although we exerted no pressure for them to do so, I believe they all did.) The only people who gave up their paychecks entirely were the members of the board of directors and the top executive officers, who voluntarily gave up their pay in the fourth quarter of 2001 to help ensure that we would have sufficient cash to meet our other obligations.

While other airlines furloughed and fired more than 100,000 employees, the employees of Southwest Airlines continued to enjoy job security, and none lost their jobs because of September 11 or the devastated airline economy. As we scrambled to protect our cash, we continued throughout the rest of September to offer our customers unconditional refunds, with no questions asked, no penalties, and no refund or exchange fees, regardless of what kind of ticket they had. While other airlines grounded hundreds of airplanes and wrote off hundreds of millions of dollars of their shareholders' assets, Southwest continued to fly all of our airplanes and to pay all of our bills on time.

At Southwest Airlines, we sometimes talked about the Golden Rule, which we believed to be a pretty good rule for dealing with each other. We weren't trying to preach religious beliefs, although it does reflect a core principle of all of the world's great religions and philosophies. It teaches that we should try to treat other people the way we would like to be treated. I believe we practiced the Golden Rule with respect to our employees, our customers, and our shareholders in the aftermath of September 11.

How did our customers respond? The anticipated flood of refund requests simply never came. On the contrary, many people called and wrote offering to send us money or forego their refunds, saying they knew we needed the money more than they did. A lot of them would tell moving stories of how Southwest had touched their lives. Some had met their husband or wife while flying on a Southwest flight; others had used our low fares to keep their romance alive when they were forced to work or live in separate cities. Some told us of how they appreciated the way our employees accommodated their children when they were flying; others told us stories of how our employees had provided exceptional care for an elderly parent.

When I recounted some of these stories to one hard-nosed aviation reporter who was interviewing me, he put down his pad and started to tell me a story. He told me how his son had saved his allowance for a year so that he could fly to Arkansas to visit his grandmother. He managed to save enough money to buy one of Southwest's $29 tickets to Little Rock, along with a $29 return ticket. It turned out to be the boy's last visit with the reporter's mother, who unexpectedly passed away shortly thereafter. I looked up and saw that this resolute journalist had tears in his eyes as he told me how his son would always remember the time he spent on his last visit with his grandmother. Such a thing would never have been possible on a reporter's salary, he told me, if it weren't for Southwest Airlines. It was because of such stories that customers rallied to our support.

To encourage people to fly again, we cut our already low fares and offered some incredible bargains during the months of October, November, and December 2001. We knew that making money wasn't our primary goal at that point. We had to restore public confidence in the nation's air transportation system and to get people into the habit of flying again. And our customers decided to defy the terrorists by climbing back onboard. While other airlines reported precipitous declines in traffic, Southwest's revenue passenger miles for the fourth quarter of 2001 dropped by only one-half of 1 percent from year-earlier levels.

How did our shareholders respond? Of the many shareholders with whom I spoke after September 11, not a single one told me that we should have followed the herd by grounding airplanes, furloughing and firing employees, holding on to our customers' money as long as we could, or withholding our employees' profit-sharing money. On the contrary, many told me that they fully understood and supported our decisions. Both large and small investors told me that they understood our culture and, in fact, they considered it our most unique and powerful competitive advantage. These long-time investors fully expected that, when confronted with a crisis, we would risk near term profits to maintain trust with our employees and customers. While the value of Southwest stock was indisputably affected by 9/11 and its aftermath, investors nonetheless gave Southwest the highest market capitalization of any airline in the world. In fact, for an extended period of time, the market value of Southwest was greater than that of all the other major airlines combined.

And how did our employees respond? Faced with a continuing flow of ever-changing new federal security requirements, our people somehow figured out how to do things we had never done before—things any rational person would have said we couldn't do in the time frames required. Yet time after time, our people figured out how to do it, often implementing sweeping changes on an overnight basis. Many of our employees worked around the clock, pitching in and doing whatever was required. Many offered to take pay cuts or work without pay, but we did not allow it for anybody below the officer rank.

During this period, we happened to be in contract negotiations with the union representing our mechanics and aircraft appearance technicians. One day, during a break in negotiations, a couple of our Phoenix mechanics who were on the union's negotiating committee approached me in the hallway and took me aside. They told me quietly how much they appreciated everything the company had done to protect our employees during these difficult times. And they appreciated the fact that I had given up my paycheck, while not asking them to give up theirs. I told them that, in truth, it had been a sobering and humbling experience. Fortunately, my family had savings on which we could draw when I gave up my paycheck. But every time we took money from our savings to pay our house payment, car payment, utility bills, and so forth, it made me think of the thousands of airline employees who had lost their jobs and who had no savings on which to draw.

After a moment of somber silence, one of the mechanics said, "We were those guys." Both had been mechanics for America West when that airline went bankrupt in 1991. Suddenly, they had no paychecks. They had been in danger of losing their homes, their automobiles, and everything else. They knew what the furloughed employees at other airlines were going through, and they were as determined as I was to see that it never happened at Southwest.

Through the loyalty of customers and employees, Southwest Airlines pulled off a near miracle and actually made a profit in the fourth quarter of 2001. While other major airlines reported losses totaling billions of dollars, Southwest reported its twenty-ninth consecutive year of profitability in 2001. It has extended that unprecedented record every year since.

Some time later, I was telling one of our employees how grateful I was to all of the people who had built Southwest over the 30 years since its first flight in 1971. I was sure the executives of the other major airlines did not want to ground their airplanes or lay off their employees. They simply did what they felt they had to do to try to save their companies.

At Southwest, we had choices. We had the lowest cost structure and the strongest balance sheet in the airline industry. We had access to cash, and we had modest debt. Our people had always followed the teachings of our cofounder, Herb Kelleher, to manage our business in good times so that we could succeed in bad times. We did not spend profligately when we made a profit, so we did not have to cut jobs when the going got tough. Our employees had always maintained their reverence for the customers who signed our paychecks. Customers responded with loyal support. Shareholders appreciated all of this and understood the value of our culture. As tough as it had been after 9/11, and as heroic as the performance of our employees had been, I really thought we owed our success to all the people who had built our airline the right way over the previous 30 years.

The employee with whom I was talking pondered this for moment. Finally, she said, "It's like my daddy used to tell me. The question was answered before it was asked."

Indeed, the question was answered before it was asked. Our people had built a house of bricks, while others had built theirs of straw. Thirty years of doing things the right way had given us the strength to do the right things during the worst crisis in the history of aviation.

Chapter 4

...But I Don't Want to Be a Corporate Bureaucrat

Before my three years as CEO of Southwest Airlines, I had the opportunity to serve as a lawyer for the airline, first as outside counsel and then for 15 years as vice president and General Counsel. In many ways, these were the most educational and instructive years of my life. As a lawyer, I had absolutely no training or experience in managing people. In fact, I never had the slightest desire to work for a corporation or become a corporate bureaucrat. After all, I became a lawyer so I wouldn't have to work in the stifling world of corporate America, where creativity was suppressed and individuality discouraged.

In general, business seemed pretty boring during my formative years in the 1960s. Cars were made by GM, Ford, or Chrysler. The networks were NBC, CBS, and ABC (and, yes, PBS, for the eccentric few who wanted to watch "educational" television). The telephone company was AT&T. There was no Internet, no TiVo, no NAFTA. Airlines, banks, and utilities were regulated and uncompetitive. Manufacturers routinely established "recommended prices," which retailers were expected to follow. There was little meaningful competition, and real innovation in the private sector was rare. Corporate organizations were typically bureaucratic and hierarchical, with the strata of white males mostly determined on the basis of seniority. Because there was so little competition and innovation, new ideas weren't really valued.

The attitude of the era was reflected by Secretary of Defense Charles E. Wilson, when he told the Senate Armed Services Committee in 1953, "What was good for our country was good for General Motors, and vice versa." In a world that yearned for stability after the tumult and trauma of World War II, Wilson's sentiments were shared by many.

Stability, however, ultimately leads to stagnation. By the 1970s, American business seemed pretty dull to a generation consumed with Vietnam, Woodstock, and Watergate.

But Southwest Airlines was somehow different. This was not just another boring, brain-dead corporation. When I met Herb Kelleher and Colleen Barrett (who was then Herb's legal assistant and ultimately became president of Southwest Airlines), Congress was about to pass the Airline Deregulation Act of 1978. Southwest still flew exclusively within Texas as an intrastate airline, but it saw the prospect of spreading its wings beyond Texas with the passage of this landmark legislation. At the time, I don't think anybody dreamed that Southwest would someday become the largest domestic airline in the United States.

Herb was not only a cofounder of Southwest Airlines. He was also cofounder of the prestigious San

Antonio law firm of Oppenheimer, Rosenberg, Kelleher, and Wheatley. When he invited me to join the law firm, I couldn't believe my good fortune. I hadn't submitted a resume or even asked for a job. Indeed, I didn't have a career plan at all, other than just wanting to be a good lawyer. I figured I might end up like Perry Mason, practicing law and representing innocent people. At the time, I was working as an assistant attorney general of Texas and had met Herb and Colleen while working on a case. Herb didn't just work on a case—he threw his entire being into it, which I admired. Out of the blue one day, he asked me if I had ever thought about moving to San Antonio. I didn't have to think long.

Before accepting the job, of course, my wife, Pat, and I traveled to San Antonio to visit the law firm and meet the other lawyers. When Herb and I were alone in his office, as I settled into one of his overstuffed leather chairs, he asked me what my career goals were. I don't think I had ever been asked that question before. Fortunately, because I was totally unprepared for the question, I wasn't equipped with some prefabricated answer.

"Gee, Herb, I don't know if I have a career goal," I said. "I don't really have a goal of attaining any particular position or title at any particular point in time. I just try to do the best I can every day at whatever job I have, and if the time comes to move on to something else, I'll know it."

"That's exactly how I live my life," Herb bellowed, as he bounced the eraser of his number 2 pencil off his green legal pad. "Let's go have a drink."

Herb's favorite watering hole was the historic Saint Anthony Club, across the street from his office. As we settled into our seats, Herb's friend and favorite bartender, Pete Ramirez, greeted Herb warmly. Almost on cue, Pete then turned his attention to me. "What would you care for this evening?" All eyes turned in my direction. As a modestly paid public servant, I was accustomed to drinking inexpensive beverages, although my favorite (if usually unaffordable) drink was Wild Turkey bourbon. I had no idea that Wild Turkey was also Herb's favorite drink.

As Pete waited for my order, I decided it was a special day, so why not go for the best? "Could I have a Wild Turkey and water, please?"

"The 80 or 101?" Pete probed.

"The 101, if you have it, please."

Herb burst into laughter. "I'll have exactly the same thing."

In the years that followed, after Herb became internationally famous and his penchant for Wild Turkey became widely known, I was probably with him a hundred times when somebody would order Wild Turkey in a transparent effort to bond with him. People recognize a phony, and Herb is more adept at it than most. In Herb's book, being a phony in ordering your drink would put you beneath even somebody who would order a pastel colored drink with a little umbrella in it.

But somehow Herb discerned that I was just a naïve young lawyer who liked Wild Turkey. Simply being myself and doing the best I could every day had put me in place for a ride I never could have imagined.

Chapter 5

Getting Off the Ground

Perhaps I should tell you a little about Southwest Airlines, in case you are not already familiar with the story. Southwest had just made its first flight beyond the borders of Texas when I joined Herb and Colleen at the law firm in 1979. Because the airline owed its very existence to a loophole in federal law, being a lawyer for Southwest was always pretty exciting. In fact, my first big assignment was to draft the federal antitrust complaint against Texas International Airlines for its role in trying to run Southwest out of business.

Southwest began flying in 1971 as an intrastate airline, flying exclusively within the state of Texas. It confined itself to the boundaries of Texas for almost eight years because of an obscure provision of federal law. This was the era of government regulation. Through the old Civil Aeronautics Board (CAB), the federal government comprehensively regulated every economic aspect of interstate airline operations. The federal government decided where airlines could fly and how much they could charge. Competition was discouraged. Indeed, no federal certificate authorizing creation of a new trunk carrier had been approved since World War II. As usually happens when an industry is regulated by the government instead of the competitive marketplace, prices were high, service was poor, and operations were inefficient.

Southwest broke the mold. Cofounders Herb Kelleher and Rollin King knew of a loophole. Federal regulation extended only to *interstate* airlines. (The same safety regulations apply to intrastate airlines as interstate airlines, of course, so there was never any question that flights would be safe.) If an airline could limit its flights entirely to one state, it would be free of the stifling cloak of federal regulations. The airline could set its own fares. It could decide where it wanted to fly and how often.

In fact, a California airline named PSA had tried the idea. PSA offered low fares and frequent flights that never left the state of California, and it developed an almost cultlike following among Californians in the 1960s. With PSA's low fares and frequent service, passenger traffic in California exploded. The Los Angeles/San Francisco market shot to the top of the charts, becoming the most heavily traveled air corridor in the world. PSA's planes reflected the delight of its passengers with a trademark smile painted on the front of every fuselage. Happy planes, happy passengers, no CAB to restrict competition. It was a natural.

Kelleher and King saw the opportunity. The geography and population distribution of Texas made it the perfect place to try to duplicate and improve upon the

PSA model. Like California, Texas has quite a few sizable cities separated by appreciable distances. Competition from existing air carriers was laughable. The regulated airlines made their money from longer flights and gave scant attention to the short haul intrastate routes that Southwest coveted. Service was so unreliable that most business travelers preferred to drive. Fares were so high that most people could not afford to fly for personal travel.

Southwest would target the automobile as its primary competitor. A one-hour airplane ride in air conditioned comfort would beat the hell out of a four- or five-hour drive on congested highways. Flights would go frequently and arrive on time, unlike the existing service. Southwest would be reliable, with a fleet of three all new Boeing 737 aircraft. Add in the prospect of pretty girls in hot pants serving free drinks to the predominantly male business crowd of the 1970s, and what kind of idiot would travel any other way?

Although the incumbent airlines had long neglected the short haul intrastate markets, they were quick to recognize the threat. As long-time beneficiaries of regulatory largesse, they considered the idea of competition to be somehow un-American.

Kelleher and King had incorporated Southwest in 1967, planning to start service shortly thereafter. When the Texas Aeronautics Commission granted Southwest a certificate of public convenience and necessity in 1968, competition in the Texas skies seemed around the corner. Before Southwest could launch its first flight, however, Braniff and Texas International Airlines, who then dominated the short haul markets in Texas, launched an unprecedented barrage of lawsuits. They basically claimed that, as holders of federally issued air carrier certificates, they should be protected from competition by an upstart airline who might take away passengers and reduce air fares. Rather than competing for the public's business, they sought to banish their potential competitor from the marketplace.

After more than two years of litigation and appeals, the Texas Supreme Court finally ruled in Southwest's favor. Braniff and Texas International asked the United States Supreme Court to overturn the decision of the Texas courts, but it refused. The way seemed clear for Southwest to begin service.

The incumbent airlines were not ready to quit, however. Having failed in the Texas courts, Braniff and Texas International turned to the federal Civil Aeronautics Board, asking it to prevent Southwest from flying. Under the CAB's procedures, the case was submitted to its Board of Enforcement, which ruled in Southwest's favor. Braniff and Texas International appealed again, but on June 15, 1971, the full Civil Aeronautics Board rejected their arguments.

Southwest had been prevented from starting business for three years by the torrent of lawsuits, appeals, administrative hearings, and yet more appeals. Finally, the airline's right to fly had been upheld at every possible level of the judicial and administrative process, and Southwest was free to fly. It quickly announced plans to start service in three days, on June 18, 1971.

Unhappy with this prospect, Braniff and Texas International decided to try again. Shortly after the Civil

Aeronautics Board ruled against them on June 15, the incumbent airlines filed a new lawsuit in state court, seeking to start the litigation process all over again. By this time, Southwest's coffers were nearly drained. Lawyer Kelleher had become so enraged at the tactics being employed to keep his airline from flying that he was now working day and night on the Southwest case without pay. But flight crews had been hired, airplanes acquired, and ground employees put on the payroll. Any further delay in the start of service would likely mean the end for Southwest. It simply did not have enough cash to wait any longer.

Kelleher worked all night in the state law library, and the next morning he presented the Texas Supreme Court with an urgent request: Put an end to this abuse of the judicial process. On June 17, the Texas Supreme Court convened in an emergency session. After hearing arguments from both sides, its decision was unanimous. It issued an almost unprecedented writ of mandamus, ordering the lower courts to honor the Supreme Court's previous decision allowing Southwest to fly. No court in Texas could now stop Southwest from flying.

When Kelleher called Lamar Muse, who was then president of Southwest, to tell him of the Texas Supreme Court's decision, Muse at first refused to believe that the airline could actually fly the next day. According to company lore, Muse asked what he should do if the sheriff showed up with yet another writ in the morning. "Leave your tire tracks on his shirt," an exhausted Kelleher replied.

Amid great hoopla, Southwest launched its first flight the next day. A year and a half later, Braniff and

Texas International were still trying to have the federal courts put Southwest out of business. The unrelenting litigation ultimately sparked a colorful rebuke from Senior Judge Wilbur K. Miller of the United States Court of Appeals for the District of Columbia. Judge Miller observed that, in the 56 years since his admission to the bar, he had never seen a more clear cut case of people trying to relitigate issues that had already been decided. Judge Miller concluded his opinion by saying:

> It is now five years since Southwest applied to the Texas Aeronautics Commission for a certificate of public convenience and necessity. This litigation should have been terminated long ago; its undue prolongation approaches harassment.

Yes, Southwest was not your standard corporate bureaucracy. These were mavericks who were breaking all of the old rules and making new ones. But even with the commencement of service, survival was far from ensured.

Chapter 6

The Ten-Minute Turnaround

If they couldn't win in the courts, the established airlines decided the best way to protect their markets was simply to run Southwest out of business. When Southwest introduced low fares to Texas travelers, Braniff and Texas International fought back. In an effort to cut off Southwest's access to capital, Braniff threatened to withhold its business from financial institutions that did business with Southwest. Southwest didn't have much money to start with, and most of what it did have had been drained by the prolonged legal battles before it could sell a single ticket. Southwest's original route map consisted of three cities in the "Texas Triangle"—Dallas, Houston, and San Antonio (see Figure 6.1). The 50-minute flights among the cities presented an attractive alternative to automobile rides of four or five hours.

Southwest knew that its survival depended on pulling business travelers out of their cars and into the airplanes. The things that business travelers in short-haul markets crave most are frequency and reliability. If they have to sit around the airport for three hours waiting for the next flight, why fly at all? They might as well drive.

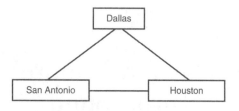

FIGURE 6.1   *Texas Triangle*

Hoping to attract more business travelers with frequent flights, Southwest soon added a fourth airplane to its fleet. As the established carriers turned up the heat, however, Southwest was bleeding cash. Cash reserves dwindled to only a few hundred dollars. Southwest had no choice. Airplanes were the only valuable asset it had. To raise enough cash to pay its employees, Southwest was forced to sell its fourth airplane.

But Southwest's schedule required four airplanes, and canceling a quarter of scheduled flights would have catastrophic financial consequences. The head of Southwest's Ground Operations department was a crusty veteran of the airline business named Bill Franklin. Like most of the other mavericks who started Southwest, he was too opinionated and independent to work for an established airline for long, so he worked for Southwest.

Franklin had an idea, and he quickly convened a team of operational employees to figure out how to make it happen. An airplane doesn't make money sitting on the ground, and airlines typically require at least 45 minutes to an hour to turn around an airplane between flights. At a typical airline, once the plane touches down on the runway, it takes a leisurely drive to the terminal, where it frequently must wait to be assigned a gate. Anybody who has ever been held captive aboard a commercial airliner while it waits for a gate knows how this annoys the passengers, who just want to get off the plane at this point. Well, it's not good for the airline, either. That's an expensive piece of aluminum sitting on the tarmac burning jet fuel.

Once the airplane arrives at the gate, passengers must deplane. To avoid a 15 foot free fall when passengers step off the plane, however, a jet bridge or air stairs must first be connected to the aircraft. This requires that the airline have an employee at the gate who is ready to move the jet bridge into place.

I have been on flights of some airlines that must have been stealth flights because it seemed that nobody at the airport knew the plane was coming. Passengers are not pleased when they are left standing in the aisle of a parked airplane, holding their bags and briefcases, because the airline couldn't get an employee to the gate to meet the airplane. What kind of respect does that show for an airline's customers? And, once again, it isn't good for the airline, either. That airplane is losing valuable minutes when it should be in the air making money, not sitting on the ground waiting for a jet bridge operator to arrive.

Next time you fly, look out the window of your airplane as you pull into the gate. How long does it take for the baggage carts and baggage handlers to arrive and start unloading luggage? What about provisioning the plane with fresh drinks and snacks for its next flight? Are the provisioning agents at work in the galley as passengers are deplaning, or does the plane sit idle while waiting for a catering truck to arrive?

Bill Franklin's team of frontline employees looked at every step of the process of turning around an airplane. And guess what? They figured out how to reduce the time between arrival and departure to just 10 minutes. It would require tremendous teamwork and execution. Nobody had ever done it before, but it could be done.

The process would begin with the pilots. As soon as the airplane was safely on the ground, pilots would aggressively apply the brakes, deploy spoilers, and put the engines into reverse thrust. This would cause the airplane to lose speed quickly, enabling it to hit the first turnoff to the terminal. There would be no leisurely ride to the end of the runway or casual drive around the airport. Southwest planes would head straight to the gate.

Since Southwest's pilots and flight attendants were paid by the trip rather than the hour, they were delighted to reduce the time wasted between flights. Southwest passengers quickly learned to expect the sudden roar of engines going into reverse thrust and the simultaneous pull of G-forces that would impel everybody and everything in the plane forward as soon as the plane touched down. Southwest's seat belts got a good workout with every landing. If you weren't wearing yours, you would likely end up on the floor.

As indelicate as it is to mention, the reverse thrust roar of the engines was frequently accompanied by a single loud popping noise coming from the rear of the airplane just after the airplane touched down. It sounded like the engines were backfiring, and passengers always wondered what the noise was. It took me several years to work up the courage to ask a flight attendant if she had any idea what that strange noise was. She politely explained to me that the sound came from the lavatory and was a sure sign that a man had been the last to use the toilet. It was the sound of the toilet seat slamming shut as the sudden braking action and reverse thrust of the airplane created an instantaneous burst of G-forces within the aircraft. I was always careful to put the toilet seat down after that.

Southwest's ten-minute turnaround required careful coordination among several work groups, each of whom had a different role. Timing was critical, and a full complement of ground employees had to be in place as the plane rolled to a stop. When an airplane reported that it was in range of landing, the call went out to all employees who were assigned to work that gate. In the employee break room, it was kind of like the ringing of a fire bell. Lunch pails slammed shut, conversations stopped in midsentence, and everybody raced to their assigned stations.

As one ground employee flagged the airplane onto its mark, another prepared to move the jet bridge into position. The moment the airplane stopped, flight attendants would disarm the safety devices attached to the door and release the locks. By this time, the jet bridge should be at the door and passengers could begin deplaning.

Baggage carts would be positioned to meet the airplane as it arrived, and ramp agents would begin unloading baggage immediately. Just as the last bags were unloaded, new baggage carts would arrive at the plane, carrying the bags of passengers who were about to get onto the aircraft.

While this was happening, provisioning agents would climb onto the aircraft as soon as the engines spooled down and start restocking the galley. Meanwhile, flight attendants wouldn't just wait for a cleaning crew to show up; they would tidy up the plane themselves between flights.

Passengers wouldn't be assigned seats; they could pick their own seats as they boarded. Repeat customers soon learned to climb aboard and choose their favorite seats with all deliberate speed. Laggards would find themselves selecting their favorite middle seat.

As soon as the last passenger was onboard, the door to the airplane would be closed and the airplane would be gently pushed back, even if some of the passengers were still looking for a seat. The airplane never moved forward under its own power until all passengers were seated, of course, but the fact that it was moving at all seemed to have a dramatic effect on passengers' willingness to sit down and buckle up.

A decade or so later, the FAA decided to ban this practice, on safety grounds, although it seemed to us to be at least as safe as allowing commuters to stand in the aisles while riding a crowded New York subway. To the best of my knowledge, nobody was ever injured on

Southwest while standing up during pushback, and we always suspected the FAA was yielding to pressure from our less efficient competitors who wanted to slow down our operations. Passengers seemed to enjoy being part of the quick turnaround process, however. They knew that Southwest wasn't in business to waste their time, or its own.

All of this required intense coordination and precise execution by employees of every job description. Station employees had to know exactly when a plane was in range so they could head toward their assigned locations. Baggage handlers, operations agents, provisioning agents, flight attendants, pilots, and everybody else had to share the same sense of urgency. They all had to understand how their jobs mattered and how each job related to everybody else's. A delay of one minute in doing any job would mean the entire turn could not be accomplished on schedule. Any delay would ripple through the day, affecting every subsequent flight on the airplane's schedule. So it became common to see employees pitching in to help each other. If there were a lot of bags to load, pilots might jump out of the cockpit and help load bags. The common ethic wasn't to "do *my* job," but rather to "do *the* job."

By shaving the turnaround time to a mere ten minutes, Southwest achieved such efficiency with its aircraft that *it could actually operate the same number of flights with three planes as it had with four.* With the cash raised from the sale of its fourth airplane, Southwest was able to buy a little more time in its fight for survival. The ten-minute turnaround allowed Southwest to continue to operate its full schedule and protect its revenue stream, even after selling its fourth airplane to raise cash. Southwest was still losing money, though, and it couldn't keep burning the furniture forever. It needed a big break.

Chapter 7

The Great Texas Whiskey War

As Southwest dodged one bullet, another came headed its way. The ten-minute turnaround gave Southwest a tremendous advantage in scheduling efficiency against its larger rivals, but Braniff and Texas International had the advantage of vastly superior financial resources. Even though they could not make money doing it, they could afford to battle Southwest's low fares indefinitely, draining enough passengers to prevent anybody from making money.

Losing money in the Texas Triangle markets (Dallas, Houston, and San Antonio) wasn't such a big deal for Braniff and Texas International. They had plenty of other profitable interstate routes, where their profits were ensured by the CAB's regulatory stranglehold. Southwest's competitors could use the profits from their regulated interstate routes indefinitely to subsidize their losses on the routes where they competed with Southwest. In contrast, Southwest had no ability to strike back. Southwest flew only to Dallas, Houston, and San Antonio. Braniff and Texas International could seek profits by flying to Chicago, Los Angeles, or New Orleans, and there was nothing Southwest could do about it because it was just an intrastate airline authorized to do business in Texas.

In an effort to maximize the use of its expensive new airplanes, Southwest scheduled flights all day long, from early in the morning until late in the evening. Fares were originally set at a flat $20 for every seat on every flight. Unfortunately, however, nobody wanted to fly late in the evening, and the evening flights were basically empty most of the time. But Southwest had stumbled upon an interesting phenomenon.

The weekly flight schedule ended up with an airplane in Houston on Friday nights. The plane needed to be in Dallas for scheduled maintenance over the weekend. Southwest's president, Lamar Muse, came up with a novel idea. Rather than flying an empty plane back to Dallas, why not let passengers climb on for $10? Although you could never make money with $10 fares, it would be better to generate a little revenue at $10 a head than to fly an empty airplane, wouldn't it? Southwest didn't spend a penny advertising the $10 offer, but word of this unprecedented bargain spread quickly. Within two weeks, Southwest was turning away passengers on its $10 Friday night flight.

There seemed to be a lesson here. Building on this unanticipated experience, Southwest decided to try a revolutionary new fare structure. Flights were divided into two classes—those departing before 7:00 PM on weekdays would be called Executive Class. Those departing after 7:00 PM on weekdays or anytime on

Saturday or Sunday would be called Pleasure Class. Every seat on Executive Class flights would be priced at $26, but the fare for every seat on every Pleasure Class flight would be just $13. Other than Southwest's unique $10 Friday night flight, nobody had ever heard of fares as low as $13. As people started learning of this phenomenal bargain, they began to show up at the airports in surprising numbers after dark.

A $13 fare certainly would not cover the fully allocated cost of flying between Dallas and Houston, or Dallas and San Antonio, over the course of a full day. But $13 more than covered the marginal costs of operating a few additional flights in the evenings and on weekends. In other words, your expenses for airplanes, airport rent, and a lot of other overhead items are pretty much the same, regardless of whether the airplane flies a few extra flights in the evenings and on weekends. (This was before the era of high fuel prices.) So why not generate a little extra cash by letting people fly for $13 at times when the plane would otherwise just be sitting on the ground?

The new fare structure caught on with passengers, and things started to look up a little for Southwest in early 1973. Texans liked the fact that Southwest was safe, fun, and affordable. The fares made flying possible for the first time for a lot of people, and they were starting to enjoy it. Flying was no longer just for the elite; it was for everybody. Business travelers loved the frequent flights and attentive service. Leisure travelers loved the low fares and new adventure. Everybody loved the time saved by not driving.

By early 1973, the Dallas-Houston route had actually begun to show a small profit. Dallas–Fort Worth and Houston are, of course, the largest metropolitan areas in Texas, and they are separated by about 240 miles of boring highway. From the beginning, Kelleher and King had seen the potential that, with good service and low fares, the Dallas–Houston route could rival the success of the Los Angeles–San Francisco route, on which PSA's success had been built. And, indeed, the market was beginning to respond.

The Dallas–San Antonio market was demographically smaller, however. Even with the stimulus of low fares and frequent flights, traffic had not yet increased to profitable levels. Overall, losses on the San Antonio route overwhelmed the slight profit in the Dallas–Houston market. But the realization of even modest success on one route reflected the prospect that, in time, the low fare concept would work elsewhere in Texas.

In an attempt to improve low load factors on the Dallas–San Antonio route, Southwest decided to make a dramatic move. It cut fares to $13 between Dallas and San Antonio, for every seat on every flight.

Well, the folks at Braniff decided to put an end to this nonsense. By now they viewed the prospect of Southwest's survival with serious alarm. They decided they needed to take decisive action. Braniff was tired of losing money competing with Southwest, and they knew full well that nobody, not even Southwest, could make money with $13 fares. So Braniff decided to take Southwest's $13 fare and cram it right up our anal cavity.

Texans were stunned to open their newspapers over breakfast on February 1, 1973, and see full page ads announcing that Braniff had cut its fares to $13 on every seat of every flight between Dallas and Houston. This was Southwest's only profitable route. Similar full page ads appeared in every newspaper in Dallas and Houston, inviting passengers to "get acquainted" with Braniff by flying for just $13. Since Braniff had been in the market for 40 years, Southwest's president, Lamar Muse, openly wondered profanely why in the hell Braniff needed a "get acquainted" sale. Other profanities reportedly followed.

Suddenly, survival hung in the balance once again for Southwest. Matching Braniff's $13 fare between Dallas and Houston would mean certain bankruptcy. Maintaining the $26 fare on daytime flights would almost certainly mean the loss of enough passengers to Braniff that Southwest would soon run out of cash. It was a seemingly insoluble conundrum.

If Southwest was going to go down, however, it wasn't going without a fight. Its defiant response swiftly appeared in double page ads in Texas newspapers. On one page appeared a picture of Lamar Muse, along with the following message, emblazoned in end-of-the world type:

Nobody's going to shoot Southwest Airlines out of the sky for a lousy $13.

Lamar Muse's signature, looking a lot like that of John Hancock, appeared directly below Southwest's own declaration of independence.

The adjacent page explained that Southwest could not long survive by charging $13 fares, but it had no choice. It had to match Braniff's predatory price. The ad then contained a simple message to Southwest's customers: If you think $13 is the right amount to pay for flying between Dallas and Houston, then pay us $13 and we will be happy to put you on the plane and give you a great flight. But if you appreciate the competition and low fares Southwest has brought to the Texas skies, pay us $26—*and we will show our appreciation by giving you a free bottle of premium whiskey when you get off the plane.*

Southwest's move made headlines all over the world. People got it. The response was so overwhelming that, for a period of time, Southwest was the leading liquor distributor in Texas.

Braniff's predatory stunt had backfired badly, and it turned out to be just the break Southwest needed. Southwest's survival became a cause around which independent minded Texans rallied. With the surge of favorable public sentiment came waves of paying customers, who would show their affection for the feisty upstart airline with lifetime loyalty. Texans adopted the airline as their own, making its success a point of state pride. Southwest went on to post its first annual profit in 1973—a whopping $175,000. It has been profitable every year since, a record unmatched by any other airline in the world.

Incidentally, after a grand jury investigation of the tactics used in the campaign to run Southwest out of business, Braniff and Texas International became the first airlines ever to be indicted and convicted for violating the federal criminal antitrust laws. In 1982, Braniff filed for bankruptcy and went out of business.

Chapter 8

I Just Couldn't Resist

In 1978, Congress noticed what was happening in the deregulated intrastate markets of Texas and California. Fares were low, service was great, and traffic was through the roof. Congress determined that the American people could no longer be denied the tremendous public benefits of competition in the airline industry. So it passed the Airline Deregulation Act of 1978, which would finally allow Southwest to spread its wings beyond Texas for the first time.

By 1986, when I became the company's General Counsel, Southwest had grown considerably. Since passage of the Deregulation Act in 1978, the Southwest fleet had increased more than sixfold, from 13 airplanes to 70. And the airline now flew to such distant lands as Chicago, Arizona, and California.

When I was offered the opportunity to move to Dallas and become General Counsel of Southwest, I resisted at first. Remember, I never wanted to work for a corporation or become a corporate bureaucrat. I was now a partner at a successful and prestigious San Antonio law firm. I enjoyed practicing law, and I liked the people I worked with. But Southwest was ready for a full-time General Counsel, I was told, and if it wasn't me, it was going to be somebody else. I had to make a career altering decision.

Because I considered Southwest to be the most exciting company in the most exciting business in the world, I simply couldn't resist. So Pat and I packed up our bags, along with our son, James, and daughter, Jennifer, and moved to Dallas. Off to the corporate world we would go.

I knew, of course, that Southwest was different from your average corporation, or else I never would have made the move. I knew the company had brilliant leaders at the top. By this time, Herb Kelleher had made the transition from lawyer to full-time CEO and chairman of Southwest, and his justifiable fame as a brilliant innovator and businessperson was already growing.

What I did not fully realize at the time was the uniqueness of Southwest's corporate culture and how an unwavering commitment to a common mission permeated every level of the organization. I soon learned that it is not Southwest's low fares that make it one of the most admired companies in the world; it is the extraordinary dedication of its people. I had quite a bit to learn about why this company was so different.

Chapter 9

Some of the Obvious Things I Learned

As a matter of philosophy and business strategy, Southwest Airlines is a low cost, low fare, high value airline. The pioneers of the company knew from the beginning that it would be easy to be a low fare carrier with lousy service, and it would be easy to be a high fare carrier with superior customer service. The art of the deal would be to have low costs *and* superior customer service.

This was the sweet spot Southwest found, producing low fares, widely popular customer service, consistent profits, and job security for employees. It became a role model for American business, creating high value for all constituencies—employees, customers, and shareholders. From its humble beginning, with just three airplanes flying around Texas in 1971, Southwest grew to be the largest domestic passenger airline in the United States. Its market capitalization (the total value of its outstanding stock) grew to be higher than that of any other airline in the world. Indeed, for an extended period after 9/11, Southwest's market capitalization was more than *all* of its U.S. competitors *combined.*

Needless to say, this success did not go unnoticed by competitors. With the advent of deregulation, the clubby life of regulation was over for the old school airlines. The menace of free market competition now endangered the comfortable profitability derived from overpriced and underserved routes all over the country, and Southwest was by far the most menacing competitor in this new world. So it was no surprise that airlines all over the world desperately began to study every aspect of Southwest's operation. They needed to figure out how to repel the threat posed by Southwest's low fares and popular customer service. In addition, as the value of Southwest's stock grew, startup airlines all over the world routinely sought to raise capital by describing themselves as the "next Southwest Airlines." The United States Department of Transportation even coined a term to describe the phenomenon—"the Southwest effect."

Competitors, academics, and analysts have sliced, diced, and dissected every aspect of Southwest's business—at least, the elements they thought must surely contain the keys to success. And they did easily find many of the obvious components of Southwest's formula for success. Among them....

1. Southwest Flies Only One Aircraft Type, the Boeing 737

Although the fleet spans several generations of the 737, as Boeing has updated the airplane over the years, the common fleet type allows any pilot, flight attendant, mechanic, dispatcher, or any other employee to work with any aircraft in the fleet. This simplicity saves a ton of money, in both training costs and operational flexibility.

2. Southwest Turns Around Its Planes Quickly

As previously described, the famous ten-minute turnaround allowed Southwest to operate the same schedule with three airplanes as it had flown with four aircraft. While heavier load factors, more passenger baggage, regulatory burdens, and more complex operations have increased average turnaround times over the years, Southwest still averages turning around its airplanes at least 15–20 minutes faster than its best competitors.

To understand the magnitude of that advantage, consider this: With Southwest's predominately short and medium haul route structure, an increase in turnaround times of 20 minutes per flight would reduce the available flying time for each aircraft by about two hours every day. Spreading this effect over the entire fleet of more than 450 airplanes would mean the loss of about 900 hours of flying every day. Remember, an airplane doesn't make any money sitting on the ground. So to make up for the loss of 900 flying hours a day, Southwest would have to buy at least 80 more airplanes. With a list price of around $40 million per 737, this comes to a tidy sum of well over $3 billion. *This is money Southwest doesn't have to spend because of its efficient turnaround times.*

3. *Southwest Operates a Point-to-Point Route System*

In the aftermath of deregulation, every major U.S. airline except Southwest opted to build a hub-and-spoke route system. This was a company-defining decision for everybody concerned because the type of route system you operate affects a lot of other things. Hub-and-spoke systems do have significant benefits, both for the airlines utilizing them and for the traveling public.

With the hub-and-spoke system, for example, a passenger wanting to go from Albuquerque to San Diego on United Airlines would be booked on a flight from Albuquerque to one of United's hubs, probably either Denver or San Francisco, where the passenger would make a connection to another flight to San Diego. The flight from Albuquerque to the hub would include many other passengers who might have connections to Seattle, New York, Boise, or any number of other cities. From the airline's standpoint, this has the advantage of allowing it to put people who are going to a multitude of destinations onto a single aircraft. From the passenger's standpoint, it has the advantage of offering service between a moderately sized market, such as Albuquerque, and virtually anyplace in the world with just one change of planes at the airline's hub.

It sounds like a win-win situation, and in many respects, it is. From the airline's perspective, hub-and-spoke systems are fundamentally designed to maximize revenues. By grouping passengers going to different destinations onto a single flight, the airline can sell more seats, buy bigger planes, and operate more frequent flights to and from the hub airport. But hub-and-spoke systems are also expensive to operate. Flying a passenger north from Albuquerque to Denver before flying the same passenger south from Denver to San Diego is obviously less efficient than flying nonstop between Albuquerque and San Diego, as Southwest does (see Figure 9.1). Moreover, the hub-and-spoke system requires massive infrastructure costs, such as expensive hub airports and multiple aircraft types.

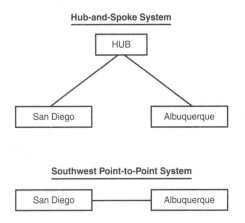

FIGURE 9.1   *Hub-and-Spoke versus Point-to-Point Systems*

It was natural for the old school airlines to gravitate toward the hub-and-spoke system because all of their experience taught them to focus on revenues. Costs were never a huge issue under regulation. If costs went up, airlines would just petition the Civil Aeronautics Board (CAB) to increase the tariff fares that all airlines were obliged to charge. Since the CAB was charged with protecting the economic health of the U.S. airline industry, it was usually fairly accommodating.

But Southwest's steel had been tempered by the competitive fires of the Texas marketplace. Southwest well understood the importance of keeping costs down, because the free market does not come equipped with a sugar daddy who will make sure your revenues cover your expenses. Thus, it was natural for Southwest to gravitate toward its point-to-point route structure, which avoided congested hubs, minimized unremunerative circuitous routings, and allowed Southwest to operate with a single aircraft type. Southwest also knew that customers prefer nonstop flights.

4. Southwest Keeps Things Simple

Southwest has no first class or business class cabin. It has never assigned seats, and it has never served meals. It does not carry pets, and it does not generally interline with other carriers. When possible, it avoids the most congested airports in major metropolitan areas, in favor of less congested (and less expensive) airports in the same neighborhoods. For example, Southwest does not fly to Boston Logan Airport, Chicago O'Hare, or Dallas-Fort Worth International. Instead, it flies to less crowded, more convenient, smaller airports that serve the same metropolitan areas (such as Providence, Manchester, Chicago Midway, and Dallas Love Field).

Each of these practices probably costs Southwest some passengers, but each practice also has powerful benefits that support the overall business model.

Southwest has never tried to be all things to all people. Just as you don't shop for avocados in a bookstore, Southwest knows that people who must have first class seats or who love airline food will probably shop somewhere else.

Southwest has historically had a clear vision of who it is and what it does. It does not try to be all things to all people. It simply tries to do what it does better than anybody else in the world. The simplicity of Southwest's operation delivers the things people prize most highly in air travel—getting you where you want to go, when you want to get there, at a price you can afford, with a smile on your face.

5. Southwest Maintains a Very Strong Balance Sheet

Despite its flamboyant image and maverick personality, Southwest is actually a very conservative company when it comes to financial matters. Southwest maintains a very modest level of debt in an industry that is highly leveraged. Consequently, Southwest is alone among major U.S. airlines in having its unsecured debt considered creditworthy by the major credit rating agencies. The unsecured obligations of other airlines are considered "junk."

Southwest achieves this status by maintaining consistent profitability and by growing at a consistent but controlled pace. Southwest has grown every year since 1973, but it has never tried to bite off more than it could chew.

New airplanes are paid for, to a great extent, out of current cash flow, minimizing the need for new debt. In an industry where most airlines can acquire aircraft only through complex and expensive financing arrangements, Southwest owns about 80 percent of its aircraft outright and pays very favorable lease rates on the rest because of its outstanding credit rating. Financiers know that nobody has ever been stiffed on a deal with Southwest. Southwest pays its bills on time. All of this means that Southwest's debt costs are very low.

6. Southwest Is an Operationally Excellent Company

In the airline business, as in most businesses, if you simply do the basic things well, you will be far ahead of the competition. I have been told by people I respect that they have been surprised to learn what an operationally driven company Southwest is. While Southwest's low fares, flashy advertising, and dedicated employees give the airline much of its public personality, it is the operational excellence of the airline that lies at its core. Southwest is consistently among industry leaders in such metrics as on time performance and baggage delivery, and it has one of the best safety records of any airline in the world. Southwest is known for its superb customer service, which begins with consistent excellence in doing basic things well.

All of these components of the Southwest formula were fairly easily discernible to the experts who tried to dissect the formula for Southwest's sustained success.

Like all dissections, however, their studies revealed only the physical aspects of Southwest's success. Dissections never find a soul. Nor do they find things like spirit, dedication, or love.

Most of our competitors missed a few other secrets to the success of Southwest Airlines because they focused only on things they could understand. Well, they weren't really secrets; we talked openly about them, but apparently most of our competitors didn't believe us. So I don't mind sharing them with you now. I assume the majority of leaders of the business world won't believe me anyway.

Chapter 10

We're in What Kind of Business?

At Southwest Airlines, we liked to say that we weren't really in the airline business at all. We considered ourselves to be in the customer service business; we just happened to fly airplanes. Obviously, this was a bit of an exaggeration. Flying airplanes wasn't quite as simple as we made it sound. In fact, we put a lot of effort into flying airplanes, and we took great pride in the excellence of our operation at all levels. But this description of our business had a point. We always wanted to remember *why* we flew airplanes, and we always wanted to remember that it was our customers who paid our bills and rewarded us with paychecks. We were in the customer service business.

When most of our competitors studied Southwest's business model, they came to one overriding, often repeated conclusion: The airline industry is essentially a commodity business. Commodities are goods that are of identical quality and are perfectly substitutable. Grain, for example, is a commodity. Oil is a commodity. Gold, silver, lead, water, electricity—all are commodities.

There may be different grades of a given commodity, but within that grade, it is all the same. There is no price competition among commodity producers because there would be no sense in it. Because all commodities within the same grade are perfectly substitutable, any buyer would simply purchase the commodity from the seller with the lowest price. So all commodity sellers have to match the lowest price and charge pretty much the same amount.

Why did virtually the entire airline industry conclude that they are in a commodity business? Because they focused on only one part of the Southwest formula. From our competitors' standpoint, the formula for Southwest's success seemed fairly clear cut. It went something like this:

1. Southwest would introduce service on a new route and offer dramatically lower fares than had been offered before.

2. Traffic would explode, as customers responded to the opportunity to fly at a price they could afford.

3. Competitors who did *not* match Southwest's fares lost customers and ultimately withdrew from the market or greatly reduced their presence.

4. Competitors who *did* match Southwest's fares saw their own passenger counts increase, but profits were often reduced because of the lower fares.

It was a pattern that recurred in city after city, time after time, and our high fare competitors were getting flat sick of it.

Southwest could offer low fares because it had always focused on controlling its own costs. Our competitors, in contrast, had much higher cost structures and would frequently lose money if they matched Southwest's low fares. This reality was so overwhelming that our competitors turned their entire attention to it. The "commodity" analogy seemed to have an inescapable conclusion: Price was the only thing that mattered. Airline seats were essentially perfectly substitutable, like corn or cotton, and customers were always going to choose the lowest price.

This conclusion led to a mad scramble by most major U.S. airlines to strip away the amenities that once differentiated their service, in the pursuit of lowering their own cost structures. Meal service went away, peanuts and pretzels disappeared, the price of drinks went up, and more seats were crammed into the coach section of airplanes. (Coach service was the pertinent "grade" of the commodity, since Southwest did not offer so-called "first class" seating.)

Gordon Bethune, who was CEO of Continental Airlines, derided the process as taking cheese off the pizza. He openly wondered whether people would buy pizza consisting only of crust. Bethune's resistance to the commodity craze actually helped Continental create a bit of a niche for itself among the legacy carriers, and it continues to be well regarded for its efforts at customer service today.

Overall, however, the commodity craze drove the airline industry toward a deplorable level of customer service. Planes were dirty, flights were habitually late, seats were cramped, baggage delivery was unreliable. Ultimately, the federal government stepped in and began to require airlines to report such things as on time performance and lost baggage statistics. Suddenly, the media, consumers, and watchdog groups had something to grab hold of, as customer service statistics became a national subject of interest. And guess what? The statistics showed that Southwest Airlines was the shining star of the industry when it came to the customer service metrics that mattered most.

For five straight years, Southwest won the so-called Triple Crown—best on time performance, fewest lost bags, and fewest customer complaints to the U.S. Department of Transportation. And not coincidentally, Southwest was the only airline reporting consistent profits.

People who had never flown Southwest were disbelieving. How could a low fare, low cost airline that didn't serve meals, assign seats, or offer first class seating have the best customer service record in the industry *and* make a profit?

We didn't try to keep it a secret. In fact, we told the whole world. Our competitors just didn't believe us. The key was our people. They were dedicated. They were spirited. They worked hard. They understood the mission of our company and believed in it. They made flying fun for our customers, and they had fun themselves. This was their company, and they were determined that it would succeed. In fact, they knew that our competitors would love to run us out of business, and they were determined to beat the hell out of those competitors.

These were the things our competitors missed in their dissection of Southwest's business model. They were not the physical things; they were the spiritual things—the soul of Southwest Airlines, so to speak.

Chapter 11

With a Little Help from Our Competitors...

I always thought our competitors did us a huge favor in concluding that the airline industry was a commodity market and that price was all that mattered. Until that time, Southwest Airlines was known primarily for its low fares. Anytime Southwest began service to a new city, fares dropped dramatically and the number of people flying increased tremendously. Thus, many people assumed that low fares were all Southwest had to offer.

In truth, however, Southwest never wavered from its determination to combine quality customer service with low fares. While our competitors crammed more seats into the airplane and reduced passengers' legroom, Southwest was updating seats to increase legroom and adding larger overhead bins for passengers' convenience. While some flight attendants for a competing airline openly referred to passengers as "the enemy," Southwest's employees continued to build bonds with customers by making flying fun.

We knew that low fares alone were not enough. In any business, low prices alone do not form the basis for a sustainable competitive advantage. No doubt, the competitor with the lowest price has a significant competitive advantage. But those low prices must be supported by a low cost structure. A business that sells its products or services below cost will soon go out of business. Having the lowest cost structure in the industry, as Southwest does, creates the basis for offering low fares and making a profit.

But even low prices and a low cost structure do not create the basis for an enduring competitive advantage if the service or product being offered to the public is lousy. Cheap toilet paper is no bargain if it gives you a rash. Cheap airline seats are no bargain if the flights are perpetually late, your bag is lost, or you are treated rudely. This is not value; it is just cheap service. Customers shop for value, and value involves a combination of price and quality. An enduring competitive advantage comes from consistently and reliably offering customers the best value over an extended period of time. In the airline industry, this means consistently and reliably combining low fares with high quality customer service.

Marketing people refer to this as brand value. Customers come to rely on the brand name as a guarantee of value—a quality product or service at a price they are willing to pay. I have been told that the brand value of Southwest Airlines is among the highest in the world. This would seem to be verified by *Fortune* magazine's annual ranking of the most admired companies in the United States. Southwest regularly ranks among the most admired companies in America. That's brand value.

Chapter 12

Leaders Are Everywhere

L et's face it. CEOs are no longer rock stars. These days, they are more likely to be perceived as public enemies.

I recall being on a Southwest flight from Texas to California. I was helping hand out peanuts to our customers. One customer looked up from her book with surprise as this overweight, bespectacled man dressed in a business suit handed her a bag of peanuts. "You don't look like a flight attendant," she exclaimed.

"I'm just helping the flight attendants," I replied. "I work for Southwest, too."

A flight attendant standing nearby felt a little devilish, I guess, and piped up, "Ask him what he does."

The customer looked me over suspiciously. "What do you do?"

I tried to evade the question. "Oh, I work in the headquarters. I'm just a trainee when it comes to handing out peanuts, though."

Her suspicion grew as she scrutinized me further. Unfortunately, I was dressed in a suit that day, unlike our normal casual attire at Southwest Airlines. This apparently made me look even more suspicious. She warily looked me over, head to toe. "You're not one of those CEO types, are you?"

Her words obviously bespoke the anger of a nation. Her disgust was palpable. I decided to come clean. "Well, I'm afraid I am the CEO," I said. "But I'm actually a lawyer by trade. I hope that will improve my standing in your eyes somewhat." She could only laugh.

It is true that I am a lawyer by trade. I know what you probably think of lawyers. In fact, I spent most of my professional career listening to every lawyer joke in the book, and I think I've heard them all. Know the difference between a dead skunk and a dead lawyer in the middle of the road? (There are skid marks in front of the skunk.) Know why couples can't get a divorce in heaven? (Where are you going to find two lawyers in heaven?)

When I became CEO of Southwest Airlines in June 2001, I thought I had finally stumbled into a respectable profession. After all, as the technology and stock market boom of the 1990s created hordes of wealthy new entrepreneurs, corporate CEOs became the rock stars of the day. Bill Gates transformed the world as no politician possibly could. Herb Kelleher brought about the deregulation of the airline industry and, through emulation, other previously regulated industries. Jack Welch set the cutting-edge agenda for the world's most visible and economically powerful corporation, and his thoughts on any subject were quickly absorbed by the masses, who hoped to duplicate his success. Sam

Walton revolutionized the retail industry throughout the world by selling high quality brand name merchandise at rock bottom prices. All of these giants of commerce were justly hailed as heroes of the free enterprise system and as cultural icons.

The world changed swiftly, and the change was not being driven by politicians, poets, philosophers, or lawyers. Rather, it was being changed by entrepreneurs. It was hardly a wonder that the highest ambition of bright young people everywhere was to become an entrepreneur—or, better yet, a corporate CEO. It wasn't just the money they wanted; it was the action. Just as many of the best and brightest sought to change the world by entering public service during Roosevelt's New Deal or Kennedy's New Frontier, people now saw that the world could be changed, and changed dramatically, through the free enterprise system. And corporate CEOs were perceived as the leaders bringing about change.

But just as I thought I had safely achieved a position that might be held in high public esteem, things went south in a hurry.

Enron. Need I say more?

Few companies had prospered from the booming '90s like the Enron Corporation. As primarily an energy trading company, it essentially produced nothing. Yet by 2001, it had grown into one of America's most highly capitalized and respected companies. Its executives had amassed vast wealth, and its board of directors consisted of an unparalleled collection of business leaders, academics, and politically connected leaders of society, including the wife of a powerful United States senator. Founder Ken Lay was one of the wealthiest, most politically connected, and most philanthropic citizens of the nation. His counsel (and money) were highly sought after by politicians, academics, and businesspeople. The City of Houston proudly named its new showplace baseball stadium Enron Field. When the stadium opened in 2000, it was Ken Lay who threw out the ceremonial first ball, to the cheers of a full house. Among those looking on were former President George H. W. Bush and Texas Governor (soon to be President) George W. Bush.

By way of analogy, the President of the United States traditionally throws out the first ball of the season in Washington, D.C., or at some other location. The Bush family was, and is, greatly admired in Houston, but Ken Lay was the one to throw out the first ball at Enron Field. It was widely expected that, at some point, Ken Lay would ceremonially be presented with the job of Mayor of Houston, or a position in the President's cabinet, or perhaps something even more fitting to his stature.

Few people knew that Enron's financial empire was a house of cards that was about to collapse, taking with it the reputations of American business leaders. As it turned out, Enron was a giant Ponzi scheme. Robust profits had been generated by accounting tricks, such as "monetizing" assets and booking future profits years before they were expected to occur. Because Enron's operations did not generate cash flow approaching the amounts reported as profits, cash had to be raised through off-balance-sheet financings, which were made to look like assets instead of debts. When they came due, debts were paid by even more off-balance-sheet deals, piling debt on top of debt. By the end, Enron's true debt totaled about $38 billion, with assets of only a fraction of that amount.

To make matters worse, Enron's top executives reaped millions of dollars in profits as the company was collapsing. When reporters began questioning exactly how Enron's profits were being generated, Ken Lay sought to reassure investors and employees. On September 26, 2001, he told employees the third quarter was "looking great." He encouraged them to invest even more of their savings in the company's stock, saying it was an "incredible bargain." Of course, he neglected to mention that he had cashed in $78 million of his own company stock over the previous 12 months, or that former CEO Jeff Skilling had sold more than $70 million of stock. Nor did he mention (perhaps because he did not know) that Chief Financial Officer Andrew Fastow had pocketed more than $60 million in profits from his self-dealing in Enron's off-balance-sheet financings.

Three weeks later, Enron publicly reported its third quarter results, and the house of cards quickly began to fall. Enron revealed a $618 million loss for the quarter. The release did not mention that Enron would also be required to reduce shareholder equity by an additional $1.2 billion due to the collapsing pyramid of off-balance-sheet debt. Two days later, the *Wall Street Journal* threw back the covers on this obfuscation. The gig was up. In six weeks, Enron was flat out of cash, deeply in debt, and forced to file for bankruptcy.

America was stunned by the hypersonic collapse of one of the largest, most visible, and seemingly successful companies in the world. As the evidence of fraud, neglect, and self-dealing flowed out, shock turned to anger, and anger turned into distrust. If the highflying executives of Enron couldn't be trusted, who could? Were all businesses corrupt? Were all business leaders crooks?

Matters quickly turned worse for the reputation of American business leaders. The pyramid scheme that had transformed Worldcom from an obscure marketer of long distance services into one of the world's largest telecommunications companies was exposed, bringing down Worldcom and sending its CEO to prison for fraud. After Worldcom came the scandal at the health care giant Health South, where the CEO and 15 other executives were indicted for allegedly inflating earnings by $2.7 billion. And, of course, the indictment of former Tyco CEO Dennis Kozlowski revealed not only fraud, but unconscionable looting of corporate assets to support a lavish lifestyle. In the public mind, Kozlowski's company funded $6,000 shower curtain and $2 million birthday party for his wife (also at company expense) came to symbolize the magnitude of CEO excesses.

Respect for America's business leadership had obviously been shattered. Political leaders were hardly regarded any better, with one recent president having been impeached over his own "off-balance-sheet activities," so to speak, and another having led the nation to war in an unavailing search for weapons of mass destruction. Where could the world look for leaders? Were there any leaders left?

I think the answer is pretty simple. Leaders are actually everywhere. They are just not always in the most obvious places. To be sure, some continue to be in highly visible positions of influence and power, but most will never achieve fame or wealth. They run small and large businesses. They work for public and private institutions. They are in management and labor. They are so-called middle managers, front line supervisors, and rank-and-file workers. They are the leaders who make organizations great by delivering superior customer service inside and outside their organizations every day.

In fact, we are all leaders in some way. The example of our behavior is seen and followed by others. We are all communicators of missions and values. And we are all responsible for the lessons taught by our words and deeds.

Great organizations require great leaders at *all* levels. The ultimate success of any organization requires consistently excellent performance at every level. Most employees will never meet the CEO of their company. Yet they are expected to share the CEO's vision and passion for the success of the organization. Where are they to gain an understanding of the mission they are trying to accomplish? How can they feel a passion for its success unless they understand their role in accomplishing it? Why should they care unless they feel some sense of ownership in both the company and its mission?

Vibrant and successful organizations are not built upon a feeling of lackadaisical detachment by employees. "That's not my job" is just another way of saying, "I don't care whether we accomplish our company's mission or not." Or maybe it's just another way of saying, "I don't know what our mission is." Either way, it reflects a failure of communication and motivation.

Every top executive I know is passionately committed to the success of his or her organization and simply cannot understand when rank-and-file workers do not share the same enthusiasm. What these top executives typically fail to recognize is that passion and knowledge are seldom transmitted directly from the top of an organization straight to the bottom. Rather, they must pass through many levels and must be felt and understood at every level if they are to be passed on to the next. Moreover, a paycheck, by itself, does not create a sense of ownership in either the company or its mission.

In traditionally bureaucratic command-and-control organizations, front line leaders are merely enforcers of rules. Today's real-time hypercompetitive world requires a different kind of leader, however. If front line employees are supposed to understand and accomplish a company's mission, they need to understand how they fit into the achievement of that mission and why their performance matters. If they are expected to care about the fulfillment of their company's vision, they must be personally invested in its attainment.

In many respects, great leadership is most important at the front line levels of any organization because this is where a business most directly touches its employees and customers. Yet, sadly, this is the level of leadership most commonly neglected.

At Southwest, we devoted substantial resources to providing our leaders at all levels with the tools for making good decisions. Of course, we were far from perfect, but I think we did give more attention to this effort than most companies. We always felt that our employees deserved to have good leaders. We recognized that middle managers and front line leaders are much more than mere enforcers of rules and quantifiers of productivity. Modern organizations require leaders at all levels who can make good decisions, inspire trust, build a sense of ownership, and motivate employees toward common goals. The role of front line leader has evolved from an enforcer of rules to a communicator of missions, values, goals, and culture.

It sometimes seems that the more I learn, the less I know. One thing I do know, however, is that the success of any organization is built on its people. And in any successful organization, you will find that good people and good leaders are everywhere.

Chapter 13

Great Organizations Have Great Leaders at Every Level

When thinking of great leaders in the business world, most people think of corporate moguls, CEOs, and the like. Certainly, it is true that important decisions affecting a company's direction and success are made at this level—choosing a line of business or a market to enter, establishing basic corporate strategy, setting the moral and cultural tone of the company, and so forth. The importance of this role is not to be underestimated. At the same time, however, any truly great leader will tell you that the ultimate success of a corporate vision depends on achieving excellence throughout an organization.

This is not a book about war, but when it comes to the subject of leadership, I think there is a lot to learn from the greatest military operation of modern history. It came to be known as D-Day, and it was the day the tide of history turned against the forces of tyranny in World War II.

The future of the world hung in the balance in June 1944. Adolph Hitler's mighty military machine had rolled across Europe and controlled most of the continent. Both Hitler and Roosevelt were secretly developing a powerful atomic bomb that could destroy entire cities at a time, but nobody knew who would be the first to perfect this frightful tool of world dominance. Unless the Western democracies could establish a beachhead in France from which to push back the occupying army, freedom throughout the world would be at risk from the madman who controlled the awesome military and industrial might of the Third Reich.

The weather in the English Channel was frightful on June 4, 1944, the scheduled eve of D-Day. Fierce winds, strong seas, and a heavy cloud cover were forecast for the following day, rendering an amphibious assault on Normandy suicidal. Reluctantly, the Allied commander, Gen. Dwight Eisenhower, decided to postpone the invasion for at least one day.

Millions of men and women from all over the world had worked for more than two years to prepare for this moment. Thousands and thousands of ships, airplanes, tanks, bulldozers, and weapons of all kinds had been built. Hundreds of thousands of troops from throughout the world had been amassed in southeastern England—Americans, Brits, Canadians, and self-assembled bands of refugees from Poland, France, and elsewhere, all willing to sacrifice their lives to fight the forces of tyranny.

Training had been intense, but most of the men had never been in combat and could hardly imagine the terror, tragedy, and heroism that lay ahead for them. Hundreds of thousands of soldiers and their massive array of weaponry had been sequestered in secrecy in the English countryside for months. The high command of the Third Reich knew an attack was coming, but they did not know when or where. Moreover, they did not consider the well-defended cliffs of Normandy a likely target, feeling the Allies had other, more convenient, points of landing in France. The atrocious weather of early June hardly made the threat of an attack seem imminent.

The weather was frightful, but if the invasion could not go by June 6, tidal conditions would require a two-week delay. Somehow, despite the coordinated involvement of millions of free men and women throughout the world, no German spy had managed to intercept the plans for a massive allied invasion of Normandy on June 6, 1944. Could the element of surprise be maintained for two more weeks if the invasion were postponed?

As the storm outside raged, Eisenhower asked the advice of the top Allied commanders, one by one. Should the invasion go or be postponed again? Opinions varied. The unsettled weather conditions made an ocean landing risky and threatened Allied plans to drop paratroopers from the sky and fly gliders that would land behind enemy lines.

Only Eisenhower could decide. He paced the floor for an undetermined period of time that seemed like an eternity to those present. Finally, he turned to his top battle commanders and, with a quiet but firm voice, declared, "Okay, let's go."

With those words, the job of the supreme commander of the Allied Expeditionary Forces on D-Day was done. From that point, the success of the battle that would determine the future of the world lay in the hands of leaders at other levels—battlefield commanders, junior officers, noncommissioned officers, and hundreds of thousands of rank-and-file soldiers who had never been in battle. They understood their mission, they were equipped with the best tools of war available, and they were determined to succeed. But the supreme commander of the Allied Expeditionary Forces could now only wait.

Great organizations have great leaders at all levels. The success of the D-Day invasion is the story of thousands of heroes who became leaders on the battlefield. As predicted, the weather on June 6, 1944, was stormy. Virtually nothing about the invasion went according to plan. Because of the heavy cloud cover, tons of Allied bombs either missed their targets entirely or were returned to base in the bellies of B-17s and B-24s that could not find their targets. Heavy anti-aircraft fire and a lack of visibility scattered the paratroopers who dropped from allied aircraft all over Normandy.

Most of the paratroopers who survived the drop were hopelessly lost and separated from their units. Troops landing on the beaches faced fierce firepower, along with intense waves, which scattered their landing craft. Nothing went according to schedule. Landing craft dropped their men wherever they could, and many men died before they ever touched the French shore.

Of those who did survive, most were not where they expected to be. In one famous incident, Gen. Theodore Roosevelt, Jr., led his troops ashore on Utah Beach, only to discover they were more than a mile from where they were supposed to land. The son of the Roughrider President, who was the first American general to land at Normandy, reflected the resourcefulness of Allied soldiers and paratroopers who were strewn all over Normandy. His legendary response to the predicament: "We'll start the war from right here."

Soldiers all over Normandy simply looked for the nearest hill and set out to take it. No Allied battlefield commander, junior officer, or noncommissioned officer of any rank called back to headquarters for instructions. Wherever they were, they gathered whatever troops and weapons they could find and began the war right there.

German soldiers fought bravely to defend their positions against the massive Allied attack on Normandy. The courage of the German troops was betrayed by the hierarchical command structure of their nation's military, however.

The German army was, without doubt, the picture of precision and discipline. Orders were followed with ferocious loyalty and courage. Hitler arrogantly believed that no army comprised of people who cherished individual freedom could ever stand against the disciplined juggernaut of the Third Reich. His arrogance was only reinforced as he watched his armies march through Europe, conquering the freedom loving but largely defenseless people of one nation after another. The highly disciplined Nazi war machine seemed truly invincible as it rolled through Austria, Czechoslovakia, Poland, the Netherlands, Belgium, Holland, Denmark, Norway, France, Yugoslavia, and Greece, and deep into the heart of Russia.

In the end, however, it was the disciplined devotion to centralized control that proved to be the undoing of the German war effort on D-Day. While Allied troops demonstrated battlefield initiative to exploit any opportunity to press the attack, German troops were essentially paralyzed.

As the Allied attack began shortly after midnight on June 6, Gen. Erwin Rommel, the brilliant commander of the German forces, was in Germany with his wife. Because the Allies dominated the air war over Europe, Rommel was forced to drive back to his headquarters in France while the fate of Europe was being decided on the beaches of Normandy.

Rommel's trusted field commander, Col. Hans von Luck, quickly prepared his troops to move from Caen, but he lacked the authority to give the order for a counterattack. Field Marshal Rundstedt tried to order two reserve panzer divisions, which might have repulsed the Allied invasion, into position for a counterattack, but his orders were countermanded in Germany. Only the Führer could give such an order, and he was asleep in Berchtesgaden. Hitler slept until noon. By the time the order for a counterattack was given at 4:00 that afternoon, the crucial opportunity to repulse the Allied invasion at the edge of France had passed. The Allies had taken the beaches, and would win the war.

Chapter 14

In Case You Didn't Get It... Great Organizations Have Great Leaders at Every Level

J ust as the success of the D-Day invasion is the story of thousands of heroes who became leaders on the battlefield, the success of any organization will be determined, to a great extent, by how it responds to the multitude of daily challenges facing any organized activity. Does it have leaders at every level who feel empowered to make things happen, or are employees essentially paralyzed until they receive orders from headquarters?

Professor Deborah Ancona, at the Massachusetts Institute of Technology Sloan School of Management and her colleagues at the MIT Leadership Center, have developed a term to describe the culture of dynamic, modern organizations: distributed leadership. In other words, leadership is about making things happen, and the responsibility for leadership must permeate all levels of a high performance organization.

Excellence throughout an organization requires consistent performance at all levels by employees who understand their company's mission, who understand their role in achieving it, and who are dedicated to accomplishing that mission. In many cases, the employees who are expected to have this understanding and dedication will never meet the CEO of the company. Their information, knowledge, and inspiration will come, to a great extent, from the immediate manager or supervisor who most directly touches them and affects their lives.

Many talented people seek to join great companies, hoping to achieve great things, make great contributions, and achieve personal fulfillment. A great organization tends to attract people because of its reputation for excellence, achievement, and success. In reality, however, the day-to-day lives and ultimate success of front line employees depend much more on their relationships with their immediate superiors than on some lofty vision espoused by the CEO.

To front line employees, their front line leaders *are* the company. If a front line leader is indifferent to achievement, oblivious to excellence, or lackadaisical toward his own job, this sets the standard of performance within his work group. If a front line leader takes ethical shortcuts, employees will see the company's stated commitment to integrity as hypocritical. If a front line leader can only recite company policy manuals when confronted with an extraordinary situation requiring the exercise of common sense and good judgment, employees will know that process is revered over good judgment.

Great leaders are required at all levels of great organizations. In many respects, great leadership is *most* important at front line levels of an organization because this is where a business most directly touches its employees and customers. Yet, sadly, this is the level of leadership at which many organizations fall apart.

The supreme commander may be the only one who can say, "Okay, let's go." But it takes great front line leaders and workers to catapult any team to great success.

Chapter 15

Great Leaders Make
the People Around
Them Better

It is axiomatic in baseball that the best players do not necessarily make the best managers. Ted Williams was one of the greatest hitters of all time. In fact, he was the last major leaguer to hit over .400 (in 1941), but as a major league manager, he was a flop. Nobody on his team could hit anywhere near .400, and he simply couldn't stand the frustration.

In contrast, Tommy Lasorda played only briefly in the major leagues, but his unique skills as a manager and motivator, and his astute eye for talent made him one of the most successful managers in major league history. Over the course of his 21-year managerial career (during which he neither asked for nor received a contract for more than one year at a time), Lasorda led the Los Angeles Dodgers to eight division titles and two World Series championships. Tommy Lasorda's talent was not in playing the game—it was in leading teams to championships as a manager.

Great job skills do not, of course, preclude the possibility that a great mechanic or computer programmer may become a great leader, but they do not ensure it, either. Knowledge of the job is no doubt essential in many leadership positions. A leader must remember, however, that the ultimate success of the team depends on other people. Those people must have the skills, knowledge, and tools to succeed, and must be motivated to perform as a team at a high level of proficiency. In other words, the leader's success depends on how well a lot of other people do their jobs, and it is the leader's job to facilitate and motivate that performance.

There is no single defining formula for leadership. Successful leaders have different styles and different personalities, and use different approaches in different situations. Some have shown great technical proficiency as front line workers, while others can only stand in awe of the performance of members of their teams. Some may be outgoing and charismatic, while others show their passion more quietly.

While styles, approaches, and strengths may vary, I believe that great leaders at all levels do have certain core qualities in common. Great leaders

1. Have a passion for the mission they are leading.
2. Recognize that the success of their mission, and their personal success, ultimately depends on the performance of others.
3. Care deeply about the well-being and success of the people they are leading.
4. Show respect for each person and the role performed by that person.

5. Are always fair and honest in dealing with other people.

6. Possess the patience to coach and teach others.

7. Recognize talent and have a knack for putting people in the right position to utilize that talent.

8. Have the strength of character to accept responsibility and do not look for scapegoats in the face of failure.

9. Have the judgment and humility to share credit in the face of success.

10. Act naturally, without pretense, taking advantage of their natural talents and personality.

Trust and mutual respect are ultimately the keys to successful leadership. A leader who is not trusted or respected will not be followed. A leader who does not show respect for other people is not likely to be respected.

People almost always recognize a phony. If a leader purports to care deeply about his mission but is never seen when the going gets tough, his actions will betray him. Or if a leader purports to care deeply about her people but starts looking for scapegoats when something goes wrong, her actions will betray her. People will not follow a phony. The qualities of leadership must be genuine. The respect and trust between a leader and her people must be mutual.

A person who focuses on his own statistics or glorification is not a leader. Leaders focus on making the people around them—and, thus, the entire team—better. I can honestly tell you that in my 25 years of association with Southwest Airlines, I seldom heard a department head describe a successful accomplishment in his or her department by using the word *I*. Credit was always passed to the people who really did the work. The word *I* was used only in reports of a failed venture.

Chapter 16

People Recognize a Phony

A lot of "leaders" think they must adorn themselves with pretentious symbols of their positions. They think they must "look" and "act" like a leader, somehow setting themselves above the people they seek to lead. They think they will be respected because they have a corner office or wear expensive clothes, or because they can speak with eloquence. But people are pretty good at looking through pretensions and seeing a person's true character.

We once had such a person in a leadership position. He looked good, spoke well, and dressed like a dandy. And he was plenty smart. Except that he thought these were the things people looked for in a leader.

As I said, though, he was plenty smart. He was full of ideas. But when he tried to implement them, they were not usually very well coordinated throughout the rest of the company.

He enjoyed socializing with and trying to impress people of rank in the company. This was a chance to show his brilliance. When one of his ideas worked, he basked in the glory. When one failed, somebody else had screwed it up. He had the lingo down. He never overtly said "I came up with this brilliant idea" or "The front line just screwed it up," but the message was there.

If he had spent less time drinking fancy cocktails in the country club and more time drinking beer with people who had grease under their fingernails or calluses on their hands and feet, he might have better understood why his ideas often didn't work. Implementing any new idea or program in a large organization requires the coordination of a lot of functions and a lot of people. He never really appreciated the importance of every job or the value of every person in the successful operation of the company.

Consequently, this person never asked front line employees if his ideas would work. He never asked front line leaders if their people could, or would, do what was necessary. And he never understood the importance of telling people why they should do something.

The truth is that if you tell people to do something they can't do, or if you don't give them the proper tools or training, or if people don't understand why they should do something, they simply won't do it. And with a distributed workforce spread all over the country, it is hard to make people do it if they don't want to.

If you want to implement something swiftly and successfully, you need to understand what people *can* do, you need to give them the *tools and training* to do it, and you need to tell them *why* they should do it. In the end, people must *want* to do it. This requires a leader who people trust and respect.

The person I am talking about never understood that. He thought that leadership was about looking good and impressing people with his brilliance. But the people who worked for him didn't respect him, and they knew that he didn't really respect them. They didn't trust him. They knew that if one of his ideas worked, he would gladly accept the credit. But if it didn't, they would get the blame. They knew he certainly wasn't going to use any of his political capital to protect them. He thought he was "leading," but in reality, nobody was following.

When this person finally left, I asked one of his former employees why she thought everybody disliked her former boss so much. She summed it up: "Because he was the kind of person who kissed up and spit down."

Like I said, people are pretty good at recognizing a phony.

Chapter 17

People Follow a Leader They Trust

Dwight Eisenhower possessed none of the personal characteristics we commonly associate with charisma. He was not particularly a good-looking man, certainly not what you would call handsome. His hairstyle tended toward the bald side, long before skinheads were fashionable. When not in uniform, his clothes were ordinary. His speaking style was far from stirring. His words were plain, and his manner of delivery could best be described as boring.

Yet something about Eisenhower inspired hundreds of thousands of men to follow him into hell on D-Day. The personal note from Ike, which was delivered to every soldier, sailor, and airman as they prepared to invade Normandy, was read with solemn reverence toward the author. Every man read it. Most saved it and carried it with them into battle. They put it in their wallets, next to the personal effects to be delivered to their next of kin in case they did not make it through the day. Some wrapped it in a prophylactic to protect it from the salty water. Many survivors brought it home and framed it.

Something about Eisenhower inspired men and women to view him as a leader they *wanted* to follow. Soldiers felt like they knew Ike, and they liked what they knew. Maybe he hadn't graduated near the top of his class at West Point, but he was known as a soldier's general.

One popular story among soldiers involved Eisenhower's early days in London. He was an unrepentant four-pack-a-day cigarette smoker. Upon his arrival in London to take command of the Allied forces gathering for the D-Day invasion of France, Eisenhower was expected to attend frequent formal events with the elite of British society. At some point, Eisenhower was told that the custom in England was not to smoke at formal dinners until the toast to the king had been drunk. In response Eisenhower simply announced that he would not be attending any more formal dinners.

As American soldiers flooded into England to prepare for the invasion, some Britons were initially put off by the free spirited Yanks, complaining that the only problem with Americans was that they were "overpaid, oversexed, and over here." American soldiers quickly came up with their own response. The only problem with Brits was that they were "underpaid, undersexed, and under Eisenhower."

Being "under Eisenhower" was a badge of honor to American soldiers, one that would soon be worn by soldiers from freedom-loving lands all over Europe.

Eisenhower's unpretentious presentation of himself connected with people. Historian Stephen Ambrose summed it up in his book *The Victors—Eisenhower and His Boys: The Men of World War II:*

> When associates, be they superiors or subordinates, described Eisenhower, there was one word that almost all of them used. It was trust. People trusted Eisenhower for the most obvious reason—he was trustworthy.

When the nation set about searching for a new leader after World War II, the idea of drafting Eisenhower for president swept the country like a wildfire. Both parties wanted him, but nobody even knew whether he was a Republican or Democrat. Ike possessed a strong belief that soldiers should be apolitical (perhaps a powerful political statement in its own right) and thus had never publicly expressed views on partisan political issues.

Eisenhower never wanted to run for office but was finally convinced that he had one more service to offer his country. He was swept to the Republican nomination and was then elected president almost by acclamation. He carried 39 of the 48 states.

The point of America's adoration of Ike is not that he was the greatest president in American history. He wasn't, although he was far from the worst. The point is that people *wanted* to follow Ike. He was not a phony. He was straightforward, genuine, and honest. He was perfectly comfortable with who he was, and he didn't try to be anything else.

People trusted him because he was trustworthy.

Chapter 18

Who Wants the "Best" People?

A lot of companies say they want to hire the "best" people. This formula usually leads to the selection of candidates who have the most degrees, those who made the highest grades in school, or people who have the most experience. Those are not necessarily the things we looked for at Southwest Airlines. We were not just looking for the "best" people according to conventional standards—we were looking for the right people on which to build our company.

As with most businesses, running an airline is not an individual sport. It is a team effort. It requires people who possess both great individual talent *and* the ability to channel that talent toward the success of the entire team rather than toward their personal glorification.

We frequently summarized our hiring philosophy with the motto, "We hire for attitude and train for skills." Obviously, that was a bit of an exaggeration. If you are hiring a pilot, for example, you want to select a person with exceptional skills and experience. The same is true of mechanics, lawyers, finance professionals, and people in a lot of other jobs. But the point of our motto was that we expected these skills from anybody we hired for such a position. Job candidates wouldn't even get in the door if they lacked a high level of skill in the necessary area, and, in fact, I think the people we hired were some of the most talented in their fields. But we were looking for more than just individual talent.

A lot of managers in the business world consider hiring new employees to be a burden and think they are too busy to spend a lot of time on it. "I don't have time to waste interviewing a bunch of people," they will tell their Human Resources department. "Just get me somebody who can do the job."

At Southwest Airlines, we put a lot of effort into hiring people, knowing that nothing was more important to the future success of our company. Every chance to hire a new employee is an opportunity to improve your team—or to drag it down. If you select well, you absolutely minimize future problems and distractions. Dealing with problem employees diverts your focus from the positive aspects of your job, and it usually distracts your team from its mission. The better you do at selecting new employees, the less time you will waste down the road dealing with performance, discipline, and discharge issues. Selecting poorly can make your future very stressful. Selecting the right people can make your future a joy.

Don't get me wrong. I'm not saying we never made a mistake. But for a company with more than 30,000 employees, we had to fire very few. On those rare occasions when we did find our relationship with an employee to be incompatible, I would usually wonder, "Who in the hell hired this person, anyway?" In truth, when we encountered problems with an employee, it was usually our own fault. We simply should have never hired the person in the first place.

Chapter 19

Looking for the Right People

Every year, Southwest Airlines receives well over 100,000 resumes, from which it may hire 1 or 2 percent of the applicants. One pundit did a statistical analysis and concluded that it was more difficult for an aspirant to be hired at Southwest Airlines than it was to be accepted at Harvard.

Nobody is hired without a personal interview, and multiple interviews are required for many jobs. Our People department did a superb job of sorting out candidates with the requisite skills and attitudes, but good hiring is a collaborative process. The HR professionals at our company were very sophisticated, and they recognized the importance of including people with various perspectives in the hiring process. In selecting flight attendants, for example, we frequently included randomly selected customers, as well as representatives of the People department and the Inflight department. Flight attendants have a very important role in the safety and operation of the airline, but these are skills we could teach them. Equally important, flight attendants are the public face of the airline in dealing with customers aboard the aircraft. The same is true of customer service representatives and reservations agents on the ground. In fact, every employee is a representative of the company whenever he or she comes into contact with the public.

As a customer service company, we wanted employees with positive attitudes and the ability to interact pleasantly with people. We used to say that we took our jobs seriously, but not ourselves. In other words, we were looking for people who could laugh, savor life, and enjoy being around other people. We didn't want self-absorbed prima donnas. We wanted other-oriented people who genuinely cared about and respected others.

By hiring for attitude and training for skill, we learned that prior experience in a particular job was not necessarily an asset in many cases. In fact, it could be a liability. Every company has its unique way of doing things. At Southwest, we had well developed procedures for doing a lot of things differently than other airlines. While we always wanted to listen to employees who had ideas for improving those processes, we did not need people sitting around complaining about the fact that we did things differently. I am sure people working at other airlines feel their procedures are superior to others, and they should feel that way. But some people are simply unable to give up that feeling and adapt to a new way of doing things when moving to a new employer. For such people, prior experience was actually a liability.

Moreover, every company has its own culture. I don't have to mention names when I say that some companies have a firmly established tradition of internal conflict and distrust. Examples of such cultures of negativity seem to abound in the U.S. airline industry. When people live in a culture of conflict and distrust for a number of years, they may just assume that is the natural order of things. Such people may be so scarred by the experience that they find themselves burdened with a negative outlook for years to come.

Don't get me wrong. This is certainly not the case with everybody. In fact, we hired a ton of great people who had worked at other airlines and who became valuable contributors to the success of our airline. In fact, they usually felt exhilarated and liberated to be in a culture where they were allowed to be themselves and have fun. At the same time, we also hired a lot of great people with no airline experience whatsoever who became valuable contributors to the success of our company. Regardless of whether they had prior airline experience, we picked our employees for their attitudes. That's how we found the right people.

In searching for the right people, we often interviewed very talented people who could make more money somewhere else. At Southwest Airlines, our compensation structure included an excellent package of benefits—superb health care, travel benefits, profit-sharing, a generous 401(k) (deferred compensation) program, and so forth. We also granted stock options to employees at all levels of the company. We took pride in protecting the job security of our employees, in granting regular pay raises, and in promoting from within. In short, our compensation structure was geared toward rewarding employees who had a long-term commitment to the company and stayed with us for a period of time.

Our overall compensation structure was very competitive; starting salaries, however, were frequently below what talented people could earn elsewhere.

This fact presented some challenges in recruiting people, but it also provided a great opportunity to weed out people who had unrealistic expectations or whose values simply would not fit in. On the subject of pay, my message when talking to prospective employees usually went something like this:

> We want to pay people fairly, but we do not aspire to be the highest cost company in the business. If you are looking to make the most possible money in the shortest possible period of time, this job is not for you. But if you are looking for a place where you can build a career, where you can make a contribution and make a difference, where you will be valued as a person, where you can have fun and be yourself, and where you can be proud of what you are doing, then this is the place for you. At the end of the day, I think you will be able to look back on your career and say that you were treated fairly and compensated fairly, and you will also be able to say that you had some fun and made a difference.

To be sure, we lost some people who chose to pursue more immediate monetary gratification. But we also hired a lot of incredibly talented and motivated people, many of whom actually took a pay cut to come to work for Southwest Airlines. Very few regretted the move.

You never know what little things may affect the decision of a job candidate whom you really want to hire. While I was General Counsel of Southwest, I participated in quite a few interviews of job candidates, including applicants for positions ranging from building maintenance workers to lawyers. I think we put together an incredibly talented team of employees, despite the competitive disadvantage we often faced in starting salary levels. Many of the people we hired actually took a pay cut to come to work for Southwest Airlines. Every one of them has an interesting story about their interview.

One of the more amusing anecdotes was recounted to me by a lawyer named Cindy, who we hired away from a major law firm. After we had chatted for a while, I escorted Cindy around the office to meet the other lawyers and paralegals. The thing she remembered most about her interview was that one of our paralegals was wearing open sandals and a toe ring. I must confess that I never understood why anybody would put a ring on their toe, but it certainly wasn't a problem for me if they wanted to do so.

Cindy found the toe ring remarkable, however. "I thought, 'Oh my god, that girl has a toe ring on,'" she told me years later. "That would never happen at my law firm. I've just got to work at this place." I'm not sure whether Cindy really wanted to wear a toe ring, but the freedom to do so seemed to define the kind of environment in which she wanted to work.

On another occasion, we interviewed a lawyer named Keila who was moving to Dallas because her husband had been transferred there. She was leaving a respected law firm in another city, and they hated to lose her. After we interviewed Keila, we knew we really wanted her. She was a top-notch lawyer—she had common sense, a great personality, good values, and came equipped with a Harvard law degree and Phi Beta Kappa key. In short, she was the whole package.

We also knew that Keila would be heavily recruited. As much as we wanted Keila, our salary structure seemed to make our chances of getting her pretty slim. I knew that she had a firm offer from a prestigious Dallas law firm for $40,000 more than we could pay, but I decided to give it my best shot. On Christmas Eve, after the office had mostly cleared out, I tracked down Keila and called her at her parents' home in South Carolina. I think I may have interrupted their family dinner, but Keila took time to talk with me. I gave her my best and most sincere pitch about making a difference and having fun.

After the holidays, Keila called to say she was coming to Southwest. The law firm had offered her a lot more money, but she knew she would be appreciated and have more fun at Southwest. And the law firm certainly hadn't called her at home on Christmas Eve to tell her how much they wanted her. The years of faithful service Keila gave Southwest were a pretty rich dividend for a Christmas Eve phone call.

Chapter 20

Interview for Attitude

I interviewed quite a few candidates for employment while at Southwest Airlines and hired a lot of great people. Here are a few of the things I learned from the experience.

A personal interview with the candidate allows you to learn a lot. If you are the interviewer, you may need to spend time determining whether the candidate has the basic qualifications and experience for the position, but these facts are usually already disclosed in the application. A good interview is not really about learning facts; it is about learning to know the applicant. Is the person open and friendly, or defensive and hostile? Does the person have a sense of humor? Does the person care about other people? The interview is an opportunity to learn about the applicant's personality, values, goals, and character.

The atmosphere of the interview should be as comfortable as possible. Allow the applicant to relax and feel at ease. You want to see the candidate's true self, not some programmed robot answering canned questions. Candidates usually come into the room mentally prepared to answer the predictable questions about their experiences, education, and so forth. If this is what you ask about, all you will get is a prepared script. This doesn't really help you know the person.

Try throwing out a few unanticipated questions that are totally unrelated to the job. One of my favorites is, "What is the last movie you saw?" See how the applicant responds. Does she go easily "off script" and remain engaged? Or does she become hostile and treat you like an idiot for asking such a stupid question? Besides learning the applicant's demeanor when something unexpected happens, you may learn something about her as a person. Don't hesitate to ask someone follow-up questions. What kind of movie was it? Did she like it? Why? Why did she go see it? Did she read the book? Remember, there is no right or wrong answer. You don't have to agree with her opinion of the movie; you are just trying to get her to talk about herself and relax.

Questions that bring out specific past conduct are especially useful. You don't want to know how the person *would* handle a situation; you want to know how she *did* handle it. "Tell me about a time you were right and your boss was wrong." Or, "Tell me about a time you solved a problem nobody else could." Or, "Tell me about something you disliked in your previous job."

How did the applicant handle the situation you asked about? Does she accept responsibility for her actions, or is everything somebody else's fault? How does she respond to authority? Can she bring forward new ideas without disrupting the organization? Remember, you are looking for specific past conduct. Past conduct is the best predictor of future behavior. Try to push the applicant to respond by talking about specific events.

From the interview, you want to learn in a few minutes everything you can about the candidate's normal behavior, reactions, adaptability, ability to work on a team, and so forth. Don't just listen for facts; watch for actions and attitudes. In describing past accomplishments, did the applicant ever give credit to anybody else, or did she do it all? Did she ever learn anything from anybody else, or is she the smartest person she knows? Does she show respect for other people? How did she treat the receptionist in your office? Did she thank the person who brought her coffee during the interview? A 30-minute interview can reveal a thousand clues to a person's character.

The bottom line is that you want a person who will contribute to the success of your organization. You want a person whose skills and talents match your specific needs, but you also want a person who brings a positive attitude to the job. You want a person who can productively work with others. You want a person who is accountable and responsible. You want a person with integrity. You want a person who will bring positive energy to the workplace, not one who will drag everybody down with a "poor me" attitude. You want a person who will make your team stronger, from top to bottom.

Sometimes the most casual question will produce an unexpected and decisive moment in an interview. I remember interviewing a woman named Kim for a position with our company. I noticed that her resume listed her middle initial as *E* and casually asked, "What does the *E* stand for?"

"You know," she said.

I was taken aback for a moment by her audacious response, but finally managed to reply.

"What do you mean?"

"You *know*," she replied firmly, as she looked me squarely in the eyes.

Our eyes locked as we sat in silence for about 30 seconds. I wasn't quite sure what to make of Kim at this point.

"Elizabeth," I finally said, for some reason unknown to me.

"See, I told you that you knew," she said with a smile on her face.

The rest of the interview was fairly superfluous. In my mind, Kim was already hired. She had shown her spunk. She had challenged me, in an appropriate way, and took control of the interview. She had demonstrated she was not afraid to take a chance. And she had shown a sense of humor.

I still don't know whether Kim has some kind of psychic power or whether she just figured that Elizabeth would be the only female name beginning with an *E* that I could think of. Either way, she turned out to be a superb employee.

Chapter 21

Attitudes Also Matter at 30,000 Feet

The pilot hiring process is an interesting one because this is a job in which skill and experience definitely do matter. Indeed, Southwest has very stringent requirements for a pilot applicant even to be considered. To make it to the interview stage, an applicant must have a specified number of hours of flying experience. Minimum hours of experience are also required for multiengine operations, jet aircraft flying, pilot in command time, and so forth. Pilots must be already certified by the Federal Aviation Administration to fly 737 aircraft before they will be hired. I think our standards were among the toughest in the industry, but we always had far more qualified applicants than we could hire. Southwest jobs came to be highly prized among airline pilots.

Within this large group of qualified applicants, we weren't just looking for people with the most impressive resumes. We were looking for people who loved flying. We were looking for pilots who were ready to take command of any situation, but who also respected other people and wanted to be part of a customer service team. We were looking for pilots who fit our culture.

To ensure that the appropriate perspectives were represented in the hiring process, pilot applicants were interviewed by representatives from our People department, by management pilots who themselves had extensive flying experience, and by nonmanagement pilots who took time off from their regular jobs flying airplanes to help select their future colleagues. After interviewing a candidate, the interviewers would make an up or down recommendation to a selection board and were expected to support their recommendations with specific points.

Two pilots, a captain and a first officer, fly in the cockpit of most commercial aircraft in operation throughout the world, including Southwest's 737s. The captain is, of course, the ranking officer, although the first officer will actually fly the aircraft about half the time. Both must be highly qualified pilots. Although most first officers will ultimately become captains when they gain enough seniority, being a first officer is not a training position. First officers have important responsibilities of their own, and they must be prepared to take command on a moment's notice.

Pilots must have a high degree of self-confidence. Nobody would want to fly with a pilot who was consumed with indecision or self-doubt. At Southwest, we wanted pilots who possessed a high degree of self-confidence, without letting it spill over into arrogance or intolerance.

In some parts of the world, airline cultures are akin to old-time command-and-control military structures. The captain's authority and decisions are unquestioned. His power (there usually are few female captains in these cultures) is akin to that of a military dictator, and the aircraft is his fiefdom. Safety experts know from studying aircraft accidents all over the world that some accidents are the result of avoidable pilot error. The likelihood of such an error is greatly enhanced in a culture where offering unsolicited information to the captain is considered to be insubordination. Indeed, several well-publicized crashes around the world have been shown to be preventable, if only the first officer had more forcefully brought information to the captain's attention or insisted on following established safety procedures.

Southwest was an industry leader in developing training programs to foster so-called crew resource management skills. While we wanted pilots who were self-assured and willing to make instantaneous decisions, we also wanted pilots who were receptive to input. There is no such thing as a zero-defect human being. No matter how skilled or experienced a person may be, there is always a chance that something hasn't been noticed. This is true in the cockpit just as it is in any job. That is why true cockpit discipline requires that even the most junior first officer or flight attendant speak up when the safety of flight is at issue. And safety requires that even the most experienced senior captain encourage such openness from fellow crewmembers.

You may have heard stories about Southwest's interviewing of pilot applicants, and some of them are true. We tended to look for different things than a lot of employers. I remember the story of one pilot who came to us with superb references and a gold-plated resume. He had great flying experience and had been promoted quickly through the ranks of the military. He had experience commanding people and had flown every kind of airplane imaginable. If he chose to stay in the military, he seemed destined to be a future superstar. On paper, he looked like exactly what any airline would want in a pilot.

Several days after his interview, when he received notice that he had not been selected, he was shocked. I am sure he had never been rejected for anything before in his life. He couldn't help himself. He had to call to see if a mistake had been made. When he got through, he was assured it was no mistake. "But why?" he wanted to know. He was told the truth. He was not selected because he had been rude to the receptionist when he arrived for his interview.

On another occasion, I was in our flight attendant training center visiting with our newly hired class of flight attendants when I received an urgent call. Our headquarters building was being evacuated. An abandoned bag had been found in our lobby, and the bomb squad had been called. X-rays indicated the bag contained wires, batteries, and some unidentifiable items that appeared to be explosives. This looked like the real deal, and it wasn't long after 9/11. We weren't going to take any chances.

By the time I arrived, the building had been cleared, except for a skeleton crew of volunteers in our Dispatch department who had stayed at their desks. The Dispatch department is the nerve center of the airline, maintaining contact with our airplanes all over the country. If Dispatch shuts down, airplanes would be cut off from communications.

As about 3,000 people stood nervously outside the perimeter that police and fire departments had set up, two brave members of the bomb squad entered the building. We all waited anxiously, praying for the safety of the heroes inside who willingly risked their lives to protect others. Ultimately, the bag was safely removed from the premises and destroyed. Fortunately, it was not a bomb.

Later in the day, the vice president of our Flight Operations department appeared in my office. We had found out what was in the bag, he reported. It was a battery-powered breast pump. "Huh?" I responded eloquently.

This had all happened on a day when we were interviewing pilot applicants. As instructed, the candidates for employment had first reported to the lobby of our headquarters building. After a brief greeting, they were instructed to walk to our pilot training center a few hundred yards away where they would be shown around the facility and interviewed. Because the training center was well removed from the headquarters building, its operations had not been disturbed by the bomb scare.

One of the pilots we were interviewing that day was a nursing mother. At some point during the day, she realized that she had forgotten the bag containing her breast pump in the lobby of the headquarters building. When she asked if she could go back and get it, people starting putting two and two together. Since the training center had been unaffected by the evacuation of the headquarters building, she was totally unaware of all the excitement she had caused. Needless to say, when she learned what had happened, she was mortified.

She must have recovered pretty well, though, because we hired her. Despite committing about the worst *faux pas* imaginable when showing up for an interview, she apparently showed the ability to recover from a mistake and maintain composure in a crisis. In fact, the pilots who interviewed her chipped in and bought her a new battery-operated breast pump to replace the one that the bomb squad had destroyed.

I think it is no coincidence that Southwest pilots have one of the best safety records in the world. They work hard, performing more takeoffs and landings in a month than their counterparts anywhere. They are respected by their fellow employees and by their peers throughout the industry for their flying skills. Like Southwest's other employees, pilots are highly trained and superbly qualified. Just as importantly, they were selected for their attitudes.

Chapter 22

Everybody Remembers Their Interview

I have frequently been impressed by people telling me how vividly they recall their job interviews. Sometimes they will remind me of something I said or something they said during their interview. When somebody accepts a new job, their interview seems to become indelibly imprinted in their brain. They may remember the slightest details for decades to come.

This experience has led me to realize that a job interview is about much more than just selecting the right person for the job. If you are the person conducting the interview, it is an unparalleled opportunity for you to communicate expectations, missions, and values. Certainly, if you are the interviewer, you want to learn as much as you can about your job candidate. But the interviewer should not miss this unique opportunity to communicate certain vital information to the prospective employee. Some important information to communicate includes the following:

1. **Describe the functions and duties of the job.** Don't sugar-coat the truth. Tell the job candidate

exactly what will be expected. Are certain skills or training required? Will travel be necessary? Does the job require long hours or frequent overtime? Will the employee be expected to bring coffee to the boss or take out the trash? Most candidates who lack the desire or ability to do the job will self-select out of the process. I think one of the greatest sources of discontent by employees comes from encountering unanticipated job conditions. "I wasn't hired to do this," they will think. When you are interviewing an applicant who you really want to hire, the temptation to sugar-coat the truth can be almost overwhelming. If you succumb to this temptation, you are surely buying yourself future problems. Every job has some difficult or unpleasant aspects, and you want to find an employee who is eager to take on those challenges. You cannot find those people unless you honestly tell them what will be expected.

2. **Describe the mission of your organization.** An amazing number of people barely know what their employer does or how the company would define success. They may not even know what role their department plays in the company's success. It is difficult for employees to feel much dedication or commitment to the mission of the organization if they do not know what it is or what constitutes success.

3. **Describe the importance of the job and how it relates to the mission of the company.** Every job is important. The person interviewing for a job in

the mailroom, for example, may not realize how important that job is. Explain that the company depends on the timely flow of information. The job of the mailroom is to ensure the timely and accurate delivery of information. Misrouting or slow delivery of information may cost the company an important business opportunity. Maybe you can come up with examples of times when the people in the mailroom made a special contribution, or maybe you have some examples of people who started out in the mailroom and rose to executive positions in the company. Employees who understand the importance of their jobs will take pride in the successful performance of those jobs and in the company's success.

4. **Set realistic expectations in the interview.** The person who gets the job will work hard. (You already told them this in describing the duties of the job, but it doesn't hurt to repeat it.) How will performance be evaluated? Is there a probationary period? If so, is there a high washout rate? What about future promotional opportunities and potential pay raises? Be realistic here. You want people to know that outstanding performance will be rewarded, but do not create expectations that cannot be fulfilled. Doing so only creates the basis for future conflict.

5. **Finally, talk about what is good about your organization and why the applicant should want to work there.** Talk about the things your organization does well and why people are proud to be part of it. You want people to come in with a

good attitude and feel that they can be part of something meaningful. If you can give your employees something to believe in and make them feel they are part of something meaningful, they will often recall their motivation whenever the going gets tough. (If you can't find anything good to say about your organization, you should probably leave yourself.)

Because people remember their interviews so vividly, the honest communication of expectations, goals, and values at this point creates the basis for a successful and lasting relationship with the employee. This is good for the employee, good for your company, and good for you.

Chapter 23

Every Job Affects Others

Most modern work environments involve multiple individuals performing different tasks toward a common goal. The performance of one task often affects others. Timing and sequencing of work are usually important. Thus, the effective performance of each task cannot be viewed or evaluated in isolation. Effective performance depends in part on how other people are affected. Superior teamwork requires each employee to understand not only his own task, but how that task affects others.

For example, in the airline industry, the turnaround of an airplane from arrival to departure is akin to an intricate ballet. Many people with different jobs perform different tasks toward a common goal. Pilots taxi the airplane to the gate, where it is marshaled in by ground employees who have been advised the plane is coming. They must be at the gate when the plane arrives, or there will be a delay.

Flight attendants oversee the deplaning of passengers, escort unaccompanied minors off the plane, and ensure that no unattended bags are left onboard. They may also have the duty of tidying the aircraft and preparing it for the next wave of passengers. Meanwhile, baggage handlers are unloading bags, delivering them to baggage claim, and loading new bags that have already been organized for quick loading. Fuelers are adding fuel, provisioning agents are restocking the galley, and mechanics may well be responding to any maintenance needs the crew has noted in the log book. While this is going on, the pilots are preparing for their next flight. They busily communicate with dispatchers about their flight plan, weather conditions, fuel requirements, and any special conditions on the route.

At the same time, ground employees in the airport are preparing passengers and bags for boarding. Boarding passes must be issued, identification documents verified, security checks performed, baggage checked, and so forth. Ground employees then assist passengers in boarding. Disabled customers and unaccompanied minors are assisted onboard, and the flight crew is advised of any special needs. Oversize bags and wheelchairs that cannot fit in the passenger cabin must be collected from passengers. These items must then be tagged and delivered to the ramp for placement in the cargo hold. As the remaining passengers board, every boarding pass must be checked to ensure that each passenger is boarding the correct flight. The weight and balance of the aircraft must be verified, all carry on bags stored, and all passengers seated before the aircraft doors can be closed.

Every employee has a specific task, and these tasks must generally be performed in a certain sequence. The timely and efficient performance of each task depends on the successful completion of others. Timing and precision are critical.

When employees understand how their jobs fit into the overall success of the mission, they can better understand that they are not doing their jobs in isolation. Their performance affects others. Poor performance by one person has the potential to throw everything else off kilter. The performance of every other member of the team may be diminished. Poor performance by a single employee may cause passengers to be inconvenienced by delays, and the effect may be felt throughout the day. Airplanes are very expensive pieces of equipment, and they are scheduled for high utilization. Once an aircraft is delayed, it is very difficult to make up lost minutes over the course of a tightly scheduled day. A delay at 8:00 in the morning thus may well be felt by hundreds of passengers throughout the day. Employees at every down line stop will also be pressed to make up the time lost early in the morning.

Employees who understand these relationships are more likely to understand the importance of doing their jobs properly and efficiently. They will understand that their performance has consequences for other employees, for customers, and ultimately for the overall success of the mission. Of course, every organization will have its own unique set of moving parts, but the principle is the same. A high-performance organization requires that each employee recognize that he is a member of a team and that the team's success depends on his individual contribution to the team's performance.

Chapter 24

People Need to Understand Their Mission

Most people probably know how to do their jobs. If they don't, presumably, they will either learn pretty quickly or be replaced. But do they really understand what their organization is trying to accomplish and how their role fits in? Are they just focused on doing their jobs, or are they committed to accomplishing the mission of their company?

A well-publicized recent incident in the airline industry makes the point. On the Friday before New Year's Day, in the midst of the heavy holiday travel period, a fully loaded American Airlines MD-80 was scheduled to fly from San Francisco to Dallas–Fort Worth. Unfortunately, the flight encountered an hour delay leaving San Francisco because of mechanical difficulties. After the flight took off and headed toward Texas, the weather took an unexpected turn at DFW. Severe thunderstorms moved into the area earlier than expected, basically shutting down the DFW airport. An on time departure from San Francisco would have avoided the bad weather, but that was irrelevant now. American's flight dispatchers scrambled to reroute the dozens of flights from all over the country that were headed toward DFW. Fourteen American flights, including the one from San Francisco, were diverted to Austin, about 200 miles south of DFW.

The airline's Austin operations were overwhelmed. American fully controlled only four gates at the Austin airport, and it already operated a relatively busy schedule from those gates. The plan was for the 14 diverted planes to refuel and wait for a break in the weather to complete their trips to DFW. But the storm lingered in Dallas. To make matters worse, the storm moved into Austin while the planes sat on the tarmac, throwing Austin operations into chaos.

As the weather started to lift in Austin, some of the diverted flights managed to escape Austin and work their way toward their intended destinations. The diverted flight from San Francisco was not so lucky, however. The pilot repeatedly requested the airline's Austin station for a gate assignment so that passengers could get off the airplane and wait in the relative comfort of the airport until their plane was refueled and cleared for departure to DFW.

Managers of American's Austin operation made a critical decision, however. Even when the weather lifted and flights resumed, priority would be given to American's regularly scheduled Austin flights. When a gate became available, it would not go to the diverted flight, which was sitting on the ramp filled with desperate passengers. Rather, regularly scheduled flights would be kept on time. While the diverted San Francisco flight sat stranded with no help from

American's Austin station personnel, American continued to taxi its regularly scheduled flights into and out of the coveted Austin gates. Several flights to Dallas, where the diverted plane was trying to go, were allowed to come and go. The Austin station's on time statistics for their scheduled flights that day probably looked pretty good.

For eight hours, the diverted Flight 1348 sat stranded on the ramp of the Austin airport, seemingly forgotten by the airline's Austin employees. Meanwhile, passengers and crewmembers imprisoned on the diverted flight couldn't believe what was happening. Toilets were overflowing. Families ran out of baby diapers. The airplane took on the ambiance of an outdoor toilet. Passengers knew the airport was operating. They could look out their windows and see flights coming and going at the American gates. Had they been abandoned?

The American pilot repeatedly radioed for help. He talked to chief pilots in Dallas. He talked to the Austin station manager. All to no avail. At one point, the captain, who by all accounts maintained his composure throughout the ordeal, reportedly told passengers, "I am so embarrassed for American Airlines."

At 9:00 that night, after sitting on the Austin tarmac for 8 hours, and some 12 hours after leaving San Francisco, the captain took matters into his own hands. Spotting an open gate, he fired up his engines, defied orders, and pulled the airplane up to an open gate. Finally, passengers were liberated from their captivity. To their dismay, however, when they finally got inside the airport, passengers couldn't find anyone from American to help them find other flights or hotels. Some luggage made it off the plane, and some didn't. Some passengers rented cars to drive to Dallas. Others stood in line at American's ticket counter for three hours, only to be told that the problem was weather related and the airline wouldn't help them with hotel vouchers. "The most maddening thing was no one from American ever approached us and apologized," one passenger later told a reporter.

By the next day, the plight of the passengers on Flight 1348 was on the front page of the *Dallas Morning News*. Within a week, it was on the front page of the *Wall Street Journal* and numerous other newspapers across the country. National television networks ran feature stories on the incident, and elected officials in Washington called for a congressional investigation. American tried apologizing, but the story just wouldn't go away. The incident did incalculable damage to the reputation of American Airlines, which has always, with justification, been considered a superbly well-managed company.

How could such a monumental blunder have happened at a respected, well-run company like American Airlines? I think it comes back to the way people view their jobs. In her book, *The Southwest Airlines Way*, Professor Jody Hoffer Gittell sought to uncover the reasons for Southwest's unparalleled success. Contrary to the expectations of a lot of people who are not really familiar with Southwest, she found that Southwest's low cost advantage was not predicated on low wages, a nonunion workforce, or inexpensive equipment. On the contrary, Southwest pays wages at or above the industry standard, is the most highly unionized airline in

America, and flies a modern fleet of Boeing 737 aircraft, most of which were bought new from the Boeing Company.

Rather, Gittell concluded, Southwest's most distinctive competitive advantage comes from a phenomenon she calls "relational coordination." In her research, Gittell conducted a comparative study of the cultures at Southwest and American Airlines, including extensive observation, interviews, and statistical analysis. Some of her observations are pertinent here:

> With frequent, timely communication, Southwest employees could respond quickly to changing circumstances in a coordinated fashion. Without it, American employees could not.

> [W]hen something went wrong at American, the primary focus of communication was blaming and avoidance of blame—in contrast, when something went wrong at Southwest, the focus of communication was problem solving.

> American employees did care a lot about one thing in particular, and that was avoiding blame for failing to accomplish their tasks. A pilot pointed out that American gate agents "were scared to death to take a delay." However, this fear generated a sense of competing goals rather than shared goals. ... Shared goals for performance appeared to be weak to nonexistent at American.

> [F]rontline employees at American ... had little awareness of the overall work process, and instead

had a tendency to understand their own piece of the process to the exclusion of the rest.

Southwest frontline employees ... understood the overall work process—and the links between their own jobs and the jobs performed by their counterparts in other functions. ... Rather than just knowing what to do, Southwest employees knew why.

Gittell's analysis clearly foretold the saga of American's Flight 1348. One of the major metrics by which performance is judged in the airline industry is on time performance. American's Austin managers and employees, and the operations center managers in Dallas, were clearly focused on doing what they perceived to be their jobs: operating their scheduled flights on time. That is the standard by which they are judged. They didn't want to be blamed for late flights. Handling a diverted flight from San Francisco apparently wasn't something by which their performance would be measured. They simply could not comprehend the impact their decisions would have on the stranded passengers or on the customer service goals of their airline. As Professor Gittell prophetically observed,

[O]rganizations that lack shared goals, shared knowledge, and mutual respect tend to have weak collective identities. Individuals do not identify with the organization strongly, and tend not to consider what is best for the organization. Instead they focus on what is best for accomplishing their own narrow task.

A few weeks after the Flight 1348 incident, American Airlines responded to the torrent of criticism over its handling of the situation with its idea of a solution. It made a new rule. Planeloads of passengers will now be left stranded on the airport tarmac for no longer than four hours. "It's a rule now," an American spokesman told reporters.

Chapter 25

Shared Goals, Shared Knowledge, and Mutual Respect = A Shared Mission

The term Jody Hoffer Gittell used to describe Southwest's greatest competitive advantage, "relational coordination," is basically an academic term for teamwork. In other words, people work across functional lines toward the achievement of common goals. Through field research and statistical analysis, Gittel demonstrated that such teamwork is not just an organizational nicety, but that it produces a dramatic difference in performance.

Scott McCartney, respected airline columnist and reporter for the *Wall Street Journal,* covered the saga of American's diverted Flight 1348, which was left stranded on the Austin tarmac for eight hours with no food, no water, and overflowing toilets while American's Austin employees tended to other duties. In responding to a torrent of angry e-mails from readers who were outraged over the blunder, McCartney noted that he also received some e-mails from readers who had encountered extended weather-related delays on Southwest Airlines. What seemed remarkable, however, was that in recounting their experiences, those readers rallied to the defense of their airline. One reader who had experienced a five-hour delay going to Detroit wrote:

> The difference was Southwest sent me two $50 vouchers and a letter of apology. In this case, it wasn't even their fault, it was the weather.

Another reader who was apparently twice diverted due to weather on the same day while flying Southwest wrote:

> Southwest staff took care of me and made sure I was as comfortable as possible despite the long lines and what I was sure had been long hours for them. Yeah, there were a couple of glitches, but these were taken care of in a manner that definitely put the customer's needs first. Finally, Southwest staff never seemed to lose what I consider to be one of the best things about flying Southwest—a great sense of humor. Even when they may have been laughing just to keep from crying.

Reporter McCartney concluded that things seemed upside down in the airline industry. For some reason, low fare airlines such as Southwest often scored much better than their higher fare competitors in customer satisfaction surveys. The low cost carriers seemed to have cultures that foster customer service; employees are rewarded for going above and beyond standard operating procedures, for coming up with creative solutions, and for showing compassion for customers. The saga of American's diverted Flight 1348, in contrast, was "a story about … corporate cultures that don't put customer service first," McCartney concluded.

Motivated employees want and need to understand the mission of their organization. They want and need to understand how their jobs matter and how they fit into the overall picture. They can become emotionally and intellectually committed to the success of their organization only if they understand what "success" means. In other words, their understanding must go beyond the narrow confines of their own job descriptions; they must understand the mission, business strategy, and values they are trying to advance.

Engaged employees will want to know how their jobs contribute to achieving the company's mission. From this, they can understand how their jobs are important, how other jobs are also important, and how the overall success of the company's mission depends on each job being performed with precision.

Teaching a company's mission and values may seem like an unnecessary academic exercise. It is, however, the first step in establishing a culture in which employees feel personally invested in an organization's success. Remember, people want to be part of a team where they can feel proud, feel a sense of fulfillment, and know that they are making a contribution. This is not just true in the airline business; it is true in any business.

My first paying job in high school was working at Sandy's hamburger stand, where we sold hamburgers for 15¢, cheeseburgers for 19¢, and french fries for 15¢. We received repeated compliments from customers on our french fries. Many people thought we had the best french fries in town, and we took a lot of pride in serving them piping hot with our burgers. The business mission of Sandy's hamburgers might have been described as follows:

Our mission is to deliver freshly prepared, high quality meals to our customers quickly and affordably. In order to keep our prices low, we must efficiently serve a large number of customers, and we must minimize waste.

During peak business hours, we would usually have a person who was primarily responsible for preparing french fries, and that person had to be very good at preparing deliciously crisp, properly salted french fries every time. A french fry chef who does not understand how that job fits into the overall mission of your restaurant could seriously damage your business.

The french fry chef must first understand that your restaurant's mission is to provide customers with freshly prepared meals. French fries are part of the meal, and they must be ready exactly when the rest of the meal is ready. Otherwise, the entire meal will not be freshly prepared, and you will have failed to achieve your mission. If the french fries are ready too soon, they will be cold and unappetizing by the time they are delivered to the customer. If they are late, the remainder of the meal will not be fresh when the customer receives it.

Additionally, a delay in french fries may back up customer service at the drive-through window, causing other orders to lose their freshness while customers sit in line. Potential customers who see the backed-up line at the drive-through window could decide to drive on to the next fast food restaurant down the road. You cannot serve a large number of customers if the line is blocked by people waiting on french fries.

If the french fry chef tries to solve this problem by cooking french fries continuously, she will frequently have an excess. The excess fries would then either sit in the warmer until they were served to unlucky customers or be thrown away as waste. Either outcome would be contrary to your mission.

The french fry chef is far more likely to deliver fresh french fries at exactly the right time if she understands three things:

1. The mission of your restaurant

2. How her job contributes to it

3. How her job relates to other jobs in accomplishing the mission

A french fry chef who understands the mission of your business and how her job fits into it will know that her job is more complicated than just cooking

good french fries. She will know that she must produce fresh french fries exactly when the remainder of
the customer's order is ready, and she must avoid
waste. She will know that she must be constantly
aware of the circumstances around her, that she
must use her judgment, and that she must anticipate
the future. How many people are in line? Are more
cars pulling into the parking lot? Is the grill operating
efficiently, or are orders coming out slowly? What
time of day is it? Will customers keep pouring in for
another hour, or is the rush about to end?

If she understands these things, and if every other
employee in the restaurant has a similar understanding and performs with equal precision, you will
accomplish your mission. You will avoid waste. You
will avoid delays. You will be able to serve large numbers of customers. And you will give your customers
what they want—freshly prepared, high quality meals,
served quickly and affordably.

Teamwork across functional boundaries, by employees who understand how their performance affects the
overall mission of their organization, produces
improved efficiency at every step of the process. Many
organizational practices involve a tradeoff between productivity and customer service, or between cost and
quality. Corporate managers are accustomed to making
these choices on a daily basis in an effort to enhance the
profitability of their companies. And customers, unfortunately, are accustomed to experiencing the consequences. Reducing the amount of coffee in a can may

reduce the producer's cost, but it also reduces the value customers receive. Replacing live customer service representatives with computer-generated voices telling callers to push buttons on their telephones may save money, but it frustrates customers who just want somebody to answer a question.

By contrast, Jody Hoffer Gittell demonstrated, through field research and statistical analysis, that the teamwork among employees that she calls "relational coordination" simultaneously produces greater employee productivity and better customer service. *Relational coordination thus becomes the Holy Grail of management practices.* It improves productivity and quality at the same time. In other words, it produces higher quality customer service at a lower cost.

Gittell found that high levels of teamwork are achieved through a culture that features shared goals, shared knowledge, and mutual respect. To achieve meaningful results, these qualities must permeate an organization, from top to bottom. Employees at all levels must understand the mission of the company and their role in accomplishing it. They must understand and respect the role of other employees in accomplishing this mission and know how their actions affect the performance of others. And, of course, they must be committed to the successful accomplishment of that mission.

Chapter 26

Do People Think Like
Employees or Owners?

Did you ever notice how people respond when you ask where they work? Do they say, "I work at a department store" and try to change the subject? Or do they say, "I'm a greeter at Wal-Mart, and I've never had more fun"?

People want to be on a team where they can be proud, feel a sense of fulfillment, and know that they are making a contribution. People want to be part of an organization where they feel valued and respected. People want to be part of something meaningful.

A few years ago, our company had a perfect attendance contest in which we randomly selected prize winners from among the people who came to work every day for a specified period of time. One of the winners was an employee named Mary, who worked as a secretary in the headquarters. Of course, Mary didn't need a contest to motivate her to come to work every day. She had been doing that for years. But on this day, Mary won a brand new Ford Expedition, worth more than her regular annual salary. And the company even paid the income tax she would have otherwise owed on her winnings.

There could not have been a more deserving or a more grateful winner than Mary. Everybody was thrilled for Mary because she was such a perfect embodiment of the spirit of Southwest Airlines. She was just one of those unassuming people who took great pride in what we did and never expected to be singled out for any personal recognition. She certainly didn't expect to be awarded a new Ford Expedition.

Mary proudly drove the new vehicle to her child's Little League game the next weekend. As she watched the game, one of the other parents asked where she had gotten the expensive new vehicle. "My employer gave it to me," Mary said matter-of-factly.

The questioner responded with stunned silence. After a few moments, he shook his head and said, "Well, of course they did. You work at Southwest Airlines, don't you?"

When Mary told me the story with a laugh, I felt proud. I was proud to be part of a company that was known not just for its unparalleled financial success, but for treating its people with such extraordinary appreciation. I think Mary felt the same way.

A couple of years later, I was walking through Mary's work area and noticed that she looked tired and distressed. When I asked her what was the matter, she told me that her husband had been mowing the lawn the previous evening when he'd suffered a heart attack. She had rushed him to the hospital, where she spent a sleepless night before showing up for work that morning.

"My God. What are you doing here?" I exclaimed in disbelief. "You need to be home, or at the hospital with Phil." I knew how devoted Mary and Phil were to each other, and I knew Mary had to be suffering great anxiety, even as she tried to keep up a brave front.

"Well, it was just a mild heart attack," she said. "Phil is resting in ICU, and I had some work I promised to get out today, so I needed to come in."

"I appreciate your dedication, but you need to be with your family," I ordered. "We'll find somebody to take care of your work, so get out of here. Just let us know how Phil is doing."

Fortunately, Phil recovered from his heart attack. And Mary still shows up for work every day, where she is a valued member of a successful team. Mary knew that her job was important and that she was contributing to the success of her company. She felt a sense of ownership and pride.

In today's competitive, customer service driven economy, it is no longer enough for employees simply to "do their jobs." Obviously, we don't want employees to come to work while their husbands are in Intensive Care recovering from a heart attack the night before, but successful organizations today do require engaged employees who no longer just feel, "This is my job." Instead, employees of the best companies demonstrate through word and deed an attitude, "This is my company."

Employees who understand the connection between their personal success and the success of their organization will not just "do their jobs." Rather, they will use their energy to make the organization better and more successful. Employees who feel they have a voice in the future of their company will not remain passive when they see waste or inefficiency. Rather, they will use their talents to develop improved processes and solutions. Employees who feel valued will not just "handle" customers. Instead, they will share their passion with customers and deliver the kind of extraordinary customer service that will set your organization apart from the competition.

Most companies probably cannot afford to give every employee a new car, but a lot of less expensive things can let employees know their jobs are important and inspire a sense of ownership. For starters, simply telling someone they did a good job, or that they are appreciated, does wonders for people's attitudes.

The goal of any leader should be to make the people around him or her feel a sense of ownership in their mission. Leaders who can create a sense of ownership and pride will have accomplished most of what they need to do as leaders. They will have unleashed the pride, passion, and creativity of their employees. The rest will be easy.

Chapter 27

Making Employees Owners

One of the smartest and best things Southwest Airlines ever did was to share its success with its employees. The first year Southwest made a profit, in 1973, it celebrated its good fortune by creating the first employee profit-sharing plan in the airline industry. The airline made only $175,000 that year, but it chose to share what it made with its employees. Every year since, the company has shared a significant portion of its profits with its employees. The amount is determined by a formula based on pretax operating profit, and it is usually equivalent to about 25–30 percent of the company's net profit every year. From a modest beginning, the value of the employees' profit-sharing plan has grown to about $2 billion. Many early employees of Southwest are now multimillionaires.

While employees are not required, or even encouraged, to invest any of their profit-sharing money in Southwest stock, they have traditionally chosen to do so. In fact, through the stock held in their profit-sharing plan and other personal holdings, Southwest employees, as a group, are probably the largest single shareholder of the airline, owning about 10 percent of the company's outstanding stock. So Southwest employees don't just think like owners; they actually *are* owners of the company.

I should note that when we created our deferred compensation 401(k) plan (including a generous contribution by the company that matches employees' own contributions), we did not include Southwest stock as an investment option. While we wanted our employees to have an opportunity to invest in the company, we did not want their enthusiasm to result in an overly concentrated investment of their assets in company stock. We did offer employees other opportunities to share in the company's success, however. For example, we gave all nonexecutive employees the opportunity to purchase Southwest stock at a 10 percent discount to the market price through a payroll deduction program.

Our employees enthusiastically embraced their roles as owners. In 1994, at a time when the company needed to conserve cash for growth and intense competitive battles, Southwest pilots negotiated an unprecedented ten-year contract. The pilots agreed to a five-year freeze in their pay rates in return for stock options.

Stock options are a perk traditionally reserved for a company's top executives. As the value of a company's stock goes up, the value of the options creates wealth for the option holder. Stock options have been the source of great wealth for a lot of corporate executives, but they had never before been made available to rank-and-file workers. The idea was so novel that at first we were not even sure we could do it or how we could implement it through a collective bargaining agreement. In cooperation with the union representing our pilots, however, we figured it out. Our entrepreneurial pilots overwhelmingly ratified the contract, and we became, to the best of my knowledge, the first company ever to include stock options in a collective bargaining agreement.

Ultimately, every other union at Southwest chose to negotiate stock options into their contracts as well, in return for foregone pay raises they might have otherwise negotiated for. While I was CEO, our board of directors also allowed us to grant stock options to all noncontract employees, from management people to file clerks, thus reflecting our view that every job had value and contributed to the success of the company. (Sadly, subsequent changes in regulatory requirements and accounting rules governing stock options would make such a broad grant of employee stock options prohibitively expensive and difficult today.)

Offering employees opportunities to become actual owners of company stock is certainly a powerful way to create a sense of ownership. A true sense of ownership requires more, however. In 1994, when United Airlines traded majority ownership of its company to employees in return for pay concessions, the transaction was hailed as a landmark experiment in employee ownership. A new era of labor-management cooperation was universally anticipated. Experts predicted that the deal would change the landscape of American business.

The grand experiment in employee ownership ended in disaster eight years later, however, when the company filed for bankruptcy in December 2002. What went wrong?

Certainly, the tragedy of 9/11 accelerated United's demise, but it did not cause it. United was in a financial tailspin well before 9/11, and its downward spiral was being fueled by employee conflict, poor service, and an out of control cost structure. In the first half of 2001, United lost $605 million. When terrorists turned commercial airplanes into guided missiles on September 11 of that year, United was so weakened that it simply could not withstand the resulting precipitous drop in passenger demand. Despite massive furloughs and cost cuts in the aftermath of 9/11, United's financial losses inexorably drove the company into bankruptcy.

With bankruptcy, the value of the employees' stock was wiped out. Employee pension plans, which were underfunded by billions of dollars by that time, were terminated. Lenders lost much of what United owed them. Aircraft lessors lost much of the value of their assets. Many employees lost their jobs, and those remaining were forced to accept substantial pay cuts. The noble experiment in employee ownership ended in catastrophe for everybody concerned. How could things have gone so wrong?

Fundamentally, the United experiment in employee ownership failed because employees never felt a true sense of ownership. United was already a company in trouble when it gave its employees a majority of its stock in 1994. The airline had a long and rich history of internal conflict. Poison still oozed from the wounds of a bitter 29-day pilot strike in 1985. Employee groups did not trust each other, and they certainly did not trust management. Simply giving the employees stock did not resolve these underlying problems.

The new era of enlightenment got off to a bad start when the flight attendants' union refused to participate, leaving the pilots, machinists, and nonunion workers with 55 percent of the company's stock. These groups were given seats on United's board of directors, but nobody's mindset really changed. Pilots continued to think like pilots, and mechanics continued to think like mechanics, rather than thinking like owners.

Most managers and supervisors were unsure of how to deal with their newly empowered employee-owners. In the face of a new sense of entitlement by employees, managers generally continued to think like managers rather than servant leaders. Indeed, many in management felt a sense of resentment at the seemingly unholy alliance between the employees' powerful unions and the company's top leadership. Middle and front line managers often felt disenfranchised and alienated.

Meanwhile, the preexisting distrust between employee groups continued unabated. What was good for pilots was not necessarily good for mechanics, gate agents, or office workers. And vice versa. The fact that the flight attendants had refused to participate in the employee buyout only ensured further conflict among employee groups. The ownership groups, who had taken substantial pay cuts in return for owning the company, were particularly unsympathetic to any demands from flight attendants. Flight attendants, who already felt they were not treated with adequate respect, chafed at the slights.

Although distrust between employee groups continued, and the underlying tension between management and workers never really went away, United did enjoy a period of relative tranquility—until 1999, when it came time for the pilots to negotiate a new contract. The pilots were restive. They had taken big pay cuts, but somehow they didn't feel much like owners. Although the value of their stock had gone up, it was tied up in an employee stock ownership trust, and they couldn't access it until they left the company. Moreover, they couldn't take advantage of a good stock price by selling it, as would be allowed by many defined contribution and stock ownership plans, such as Southwest Airlines' profit-sharing and stock option plans.

The fundamental structure of the United employee stock ownership trust ran afoul of a fundamental rule of capitalism: If you can't sell it, you don't really own it.

Arguing that they couldn't eat stock, the pilots now wanted big pay raises. Rick Dubinsky, the president of the pilots' union, reportedly summarized his position as follows:

> We don't want to kill the golden goose. We just want to choke it by the neck until it gives us every last egg.

Ironically, by virtue of his position with the union, Dubinsky also served on United's board of directors, the governing body of the very goose he wanted to choke.

Despite the fact that employees now owned a majority of United, the company's management knew that acceding to the pilots' pay demands would add unaffordable new expenses to United's already unsustainable cost structure. As negotiations slowed to a crawl, and dragged into the year 2000, angry and frustrated pilots decided to take matters into their own hands.

Dubinsky told pilots they were not obligated to pick up open flights beyond their minimum schedule, as is the usual practice. The union encouraged pilots to fly "to the letter" of their contract. In other words, take your time and just do the minimum you can get by with.

With the pilots' slowdown, United's flight schedule was reduced to shambles. Flight delays were routine. Cancellations were common. Flights that had pushed back from the gate and taxied to the runway would slowly return to the gate because the pilot wanted his gauges double-checked by mechanics. Flights were delayed or canceled because a pilot would declare a plane unairworthy due to a broken coffee maker. The pilots had declared war on their own company.

In May of that year, when word leaked out that United's top management was negotiating a merger with competitor US Airways, United's employees were universally outraged. They thought they owned the company, and now management was negotiating a deal that could threaten their jobs, their seniority, and their ownership of the airline. What kind of scam was this?

With employees in open revolt, mayhem ensued. Chronic flight cancellations and delays forced United to cut flights from its schedule. Despite the reduced flight schedule, the number of delays and cancellations was still through the roof, and the schedule was totally unreliable. Customer service on the ground wasn't much better, as overwhelmed ground employees tried to deal with mobs of irate passengers. The traveling public was disgusted with United. Vacations were ruined. Business meetings were cancelled. Passengers just didn't know what was going to happen when they went to the airport. It didn't help that, on a national television program, one United flight attendant referred to passengers as "the enemy."

United CEO Jim Goodwin went on national television and apologized for the chaos, but the damage was done.

Feeling it had no alternative, the company ultimately sought peace with its employees and caved in to the pilots' demands for huge pay increases. Of course, every other group in the company quickly got in line, demanding equal treatment. United's financial viability was pretty much destroyed by all of this, and customer avoidance of the airline made it impossible to cover the cost of all the massive new pay raises. The company was already crippled well before 9/11. The terrorist attacks simply applied the *coup de grace*.

United's venture into employee ownership ultimately failed because its employees never really thought like owners. They never truly felt that their personal self-interest was perfectly aligned with their company's success. The fact that they owned a majority of their company's stock was not enough to create a true ownership mentality. Employees did not realize that when they declared war on their company, they were declaring war on themselves. The golden goose being choked by the neck was *their* golden goose. And sometimes when you choke a goose by the neck, you misjudge and choke it just a little too hard.

As Pogo would have said, "We have met the enemy, and he is us."

Chapter 28

A Sense of Ownership

For any business truly to unleash the creative passion and energy of its employees, it is not enough (and may not even be necessary) for employees simply to own shares of a company's stock. What is required is for employees to *feel* like owners and *think* like owners.

In a free enterprise economy, profits are considered the hallmark of success. Owners understand the importance of making a profit. But what about organizations that operate outside the private sector? What about teachers, civil servants, law enforcement officers, firefighters, and soldiers? A lot of highly dedicated people work for organizations that do not aspire to make a profit and do not have any private "owner." Yet many of these people nonetheless feel a sense of ownership of their missions. They think and feel more like owners than employees.

A sense of ownership involves much more than just owning shares of a company's stock. It involves an intellectual and emotional bond between individuals and the mission they are trying to accomplish.

When my wife was a high school teacher, for example, she sometimes did not have all the supplies she needed for a class project or all the resources she needed to help her students learn. So she would buy them out of her own pocket. If a student needed special attention, she would stay after school to help. She would grade papers at night and on weekends, taking time to make comments that might give the student that extra little push to do better next time.

Most teachers I know do the same things. They don't get paid extra for those things. They do them because they feel a sense of ownership in their mission. They don't own shares of stock in the school. They just have that intellectual and emotional bond with their missions. And in my wife's case, she had a great principal who let her know that she was appreciated and she was making a difference. Those words of encouragement, along with her own determination to make a difference in her students' lives, sometimes kept her going.

Most people have the capacity for this kind of commitment inside them somewhere. All too often, however, they have it beaten out of them by managers who just want employees to "do their jobs" and by companies that view employees as depreciable assets to be used up and thrown away.

You can see the results in any customer service business. When you go to the airport or hardware store, do the front line employees who interact with the public truly care about your patronage, or do they just want to "handle" you so they can get to their next break? When you call for customer service because your computer is down, does the person you are talking to really care if your problem gets fixed, or is he just checking off boxes on a checklist? When the cable guy shows up at your house, is he a great customer service representative, or does he spend most of his time telling you how lousy the cable company is and that you ought to get satellite?

I don't think there is a single comprehensive list of things to create that special bond that is so essential to a feeling of ownership, but I do believe the way a company treats its employees has a lot to do with it. This point was brought home to me on a cold, snowy day in Boston a few years ago.

I had been invited to address a breakfast meeting of the CEO Club of Boston. I was told this was a very prestigious group, and when I saw the list of anticipated attendees, I saw why. It included CEOs of multibillion-dollar companies, world-famous entrepreneurs, fund managers who controlled the investment of billions of dollars, and some of the highest public officials in Massachusetts.

Unfortunately, the night before my speech, a winter storm like I had never seen blew into town. Snow was blowing sideways all night long. When I awoke at 5:00 AM, the television said the wind chill factor was the second coldest in Boston history. I looked outside, and the streets were empty. The city was covered in snow.

At that point, I figured my trip from Texas had been for nothing, except to let me experience how cold it can get in New England. Amazingly enough, however, a television reporter and crew showed up at 6:30 for my scheduled interview. They agreed it was a little chilly but didn't seem to find anything extraordinary about the weather.

A half-hour later, I walked into the ballroom in the Boston Harbor Hotel and was shocked. It was packed with hundreds of people. I was overwhelmed, although I knew they certainly hadn't come to hear *me*. They had come because they had heard of Southwest Airlines and wanted to know more.

I started off by asking the audience how many had ever flown on Southwest, expecting a few dozen hands, at most. To my dismay, almost everybody in the room raised their hands. This was shocking to me, for three reasons:

1. This was clearly a high-dollar audience who could afford to fly any airline they wanted.
2. Southwest is a low fare airline, with no first class cabin.
3. Southwest does not even serve Boston Logan Airport, which you could see out the hotel windows.

For some reason, even though they might have had to go to neighboring Providence, Rhode Island, or Manchester, New Hampshire to do so, everybody in the audience had flown on Southwest Airlines and seemed to love it.

I told them a little about Southwest's history, culture, and philosophy, and then invited questions. After several friendly questions, one member of the audience stood up and said, "You tell an interesting story, and it's good to hear what the CEO has to say, but I notice that you have a couple of tables over here with some Southwest employees at them. I'd like to hear from those folks."

Whereupon, he randomly selected one of the Southwest employees in attendance and said, "You. Stand up. I assume you love working at Southwest Airlines, or you wouldn't be here. I want to know why."

The employee was a little startled, but she stood up and said without hesitation, "I think I love working there because it's a company that loves you back."

Well, I knew I couldn't top that, so I just thanked the audience and sat down.

After the speech, I was honored to learn that the audience had included Bob Kraft, the owner of the New England Patriots football team. Mr. Kraft, who normally attends all of his team's practices, told me that he had skipped practice that morning, the week before a critical playoff game against the Indianapolis Colts, because he was such a fan of Southwest Airlines. He admired our culture of teamwork.

When I saw Mr. Kraft accepting the trophy a few weeks later, after his team won the world championship, I was not surprised to hear him use the word *team* about six times in 30 seconds to describe the reason for the Patriots' success. It was because they played like a *team*, not merely like a bunch of very talented players.

Employees who feel that their company loves them are likely to love their company back and to feel a true sense of ownership in its future. Employees who work for leaders who define success in terms of team goals rather than individual accomplishments are more likely to feel a sense of ownership in the team's success. They will think like entrepreneurs. They will think unconventionally. They will embrace the mission you are trying to accomplish. In short, they will feel a true sense of ownership and will think and act like owners.

At Southwest, we were sometimes asked who we sought to serve first—employees, customers, or shareholders. We always said employees come first. We knew the way we treated our employees would determine their attitude toward our company. We knew that if we served our employees well, they would serve our customers well. And if our customers were happy, it was pretty likely the shareholders would be happy too.

Chapter 29

Make Work Fun

People who enjoy their work do a better job than people who don't. They work harder. They deliver better customer service. They come up with new ideas.

Customers often told me that what made Southwest different from other companies was its employees. They were friendly, efficient, and cheerful. They seemed happy. They always treated customers with warmth and hospitality. They acted like they enjoyed their jobs.

I think they acted that way because, for the most part, they actually did enjoy their jobs. Don't get me wrong. Their jobs involved hard work, both physically and mentally. The days when I helped out by working at the ticket counter, sitting next to a reservations agent, or handing out peanuts on a flight were a great education. The jobs are physically exhausting and mentally challenging. I was worn out after working a single shift. Yet our employees somehow did all of these things and could still smile at a customer at the end of a long day.

And the smiles were genuine. People are pretty good at recognizing a phony. This goes for customers as well as employees. Our employees' smiles were not phony.

What makes work fun? Some companies think, "We will have a party and then it will be fun to work here." But when people go to work the next day, it's still not fun.

Parties and banquets can certainly be part of a culture of fun, but they are not the heart of it. For work to be fun, people must enjoy their jobs. This does not mean the jobs must be easy or the hours short. People who work long days at hard jobs can enjoy their work—in fact, they probably enjoy it more than other people.

What makes work fun? I don't think there is a single formula or a comprehensive checklist, but here are a few things I have observed about places where people seem to enjoy their work:

1. People find their work fulfilling. They feel like they are actually accomplishing something.

2. People feel appreciated. Somebody took time to say "thank you" or "good job."

3. People feel they can be themselves and express their personalities.

4. People feel they are valued for their minds, not just for doing mindless work.

5. People like the people they work with, including their boss. Working with nice people is a lot better than working with unfriendly people.

6. People know their jobs are valued by the company. Fulfillment comes from within, but people also need to know that the company and the boss value the job.

7. People believe in the mission of their company and their job.

8. People feel they are treated with respect.

9. People have a true sense of ownership in the company and its mission. It's always more fun to feel like an owner than an employee.

10. People do not have to check their values at the door. Most people would prefer to work in an environment of integrity, where they are not asked to do anything contrary to their values.

11. Success is celebrated. People like to celebrate victories, and they like to be recognized when they have helped accomplish something. Even if they personally had nothing to do with it, a success for the company or department should be cause for celebration.

12. People are not liquidated for making a mistake. Thomas Edison once said man would never fly. People make mistakes.

13. People are not turned into scapegoats when something goes wrong. Sometimes this takes a leader with broad shoulders who will take some heat rather than looking for somebody to blame.

14. Credit is shared. Sometimes this takes a leader whose ego does not require the spotlight.

15. Friends and family think the job and the company are really cool. Don't underestimate this one. People can draw a lot of self-esteem from what other people think of their job and the company they work for.

This is certainly not a comprehensive list, but it is a pretty good start. You may notice that I did not talk about pay. Of course, people want and need to be paid fairly for their work. But that is not what makes work fun. A lot of highly paid people hate their jobs. Historically, some of the highest paid people in the airline industry have delivered some of the worst customer service simply because they hated their jobs and hated their companies.

Employees who enjoy their jobs will probably love their company because they feel their company loves them back. Work will be fun, and it will show.

Chapter 30

Build a Customer
Service Culture

We have all probably encountered "customer service" representatives who were rude and surly, and didn't really care about our needs as a customer. Maybe they were near the end of their shifts or their backs ached. Or maybe they were just having a bad day. Or maybe they hated their jobs.

I'm not saying this never happened at Southwest. We sometimes had customers who encountered bad customer service. Our best customers were usually thoughtful enough to let us know about it because they knew that such events did not represent our company's customer service culture. We appreciated our customers' interest in our business, and we always followed up on these reports.

Unlike a lot of companies that simply send out form letters telling customers how much the company values their opinions, every customer communication received a personal response at Southwest. We did have standard explanations for recurring questions about various policies or procedures, but every letter received a personal response. Letters that involved a conflict between a customer and an employee or that alleged inappropriate behavior by an employee received special attention. We tried to investigate every such complaint.

Customers aren't always right. In most cases, our internal investigations revealed that our employees simply couldn't give the customer the answer they wanted. As anybody who has ever watched the unscripted A&E network television show *Airline* knows, customers can be rushed, rude, and sometimes abusive when they don't get the answers they want. Most customers are perfectly pleasant, but sometimes they go over the edge. In such situations, we supported our employees. We certainly were not going to apologize to somebody who was rude to or abused one of our employees.

On some occasions, we did find that our employees had acted inappropriately or simply had not used the best judgment. On rare occasions, we found that we had picked the wrong person for the job and needed to make a change, but this was the exception. Usually, it was just a case of somebody having a bad day, being in a hurry, or having a personal crisis in their life. They just needed a little counseling and a reminder of why we were in business.

We appreciated our customers' feedback and actually found that the number of compliments we received on our employees far exceeded the number of complaints. Our customers really seemed to feel this was *their* airline, and they just wanted to let us know how it was doing.

A culture of customer service is the key to building an enduring competitive advantage in any customer service business. Having the lowest price is only the start. Customers will not long tolerate bad service just to get a low price. Moreover, some competitor will ultimately figure out how to match a low price, so low prices are merely a fleeting competitive advantage. A true customer service culture is not so easy to match.

A customer service culture starts with *internal* customers. There is one rule every leader should remember: The way you treat your employees will determine the way your employees treat customers.

Employees who enjoy their jobs, love their company, and feel appreciated will *want* to deliver superior customer service. They will be passionate about it. They will want customers to love their company as much as they do. They will value customers, care for them, and turn customers into advocates.

Employees who love their jobs will cause customers to love the company. Employees who hate their jobs will make customers hate the company.

Chapter 31

Everything He Did Was So I Could Come to Work...

A few years after I became General Counsel, we had an opportunity to add another lawyer to our department. I had already hired several good ones, drawing heavily on contacts at my old law firm. In fact, one year when I returned to San Antonio for my old firm's Christmas party (yes, we called it a Christmas party, even though the name of our firm was Oppenheimer, Rosenberg, Kelleher & Wheatley), my old partner, David Oppenheimer, asked if I was there on a recruiting trip.

This time, however, we wanted to broaden our search. Our People department posted notice of the opening in all the logical places, and the announcement brought a wealth of good candidates. Our associate general counsel, Debby Ackerman, and my departmental manager of administration, Debbie Neel, wanted to cast our net even wider, however. They decided to buy a want ad in the newsletter of the African American lawyers' association in Dallas announcing the opening. They didn't ask anybody's permission; they just did it.

As luck would have it, somebody in Dallas sent the ad to a lawyer named Beverly, who was a successful lawyer for a major law firm in Washington, D.C. Beverly had grown up in Oklahoma and had toyed with the idea of returning to the area, where most of her family lived, so she sent us her resume.

Debby Ackerman interviewed quite a few candidates for the job and narrowed the list down to a couple, who I was to interview. Once I met Beverly, it was clear that she was the person we wanted. She had it all. She was a great lawyer, she had great values, she had a sense of humor and a great personality, and I just plain liked her. Even though she had attended Oklahoma University, the archrival of my alma mater, I had to say she was the person we wanted. She wasn't just the *lawyer* we wanted; she was the *person* we wanted.

Shortly after Beverly started to work, she called the office one morning to say she had a problem and would be late to work. When Beverly finally arrived, of course, everybody was concerned about her well-being and wanted to know if she was okay. Beverly was flushed with embarrassment. She was wearing a very nice out-fit, but she told us we had better get used to seeing it.

"What happened?" We all wanted to know.

While she looked for a house to buy, Beverly was living in a nice apartment complex, she explained. As a convenience to residents with upstairs apartments, the building contained a trash chute in which people could throw their trash bags. That morning, Beverly threw out her trash—except that she had grabbed the wrong bag. When she returned to her apartment and prepared to leave for work, she picked up the bag to take to the dry cleaners and realized she was holding a sack of garbage. She had inadvertently just thrown all her nice clothes into the trash chute. Of course, she ran downstairs in search of her clothing, only to learn that it had already been hauled off to the landfill.

This happened on the very day I was scheduled to attend an executive office luncheon, where about 300 people from the executive office and other departments meet and exchange information. When it came my turn to report on recent developments, I just couldn't resist telling Beverly's story.

By the time I returned to my office after lunch, I found Beverly standing in my door. "What did you do?" she demanded to know. I confessed that I had told the story of her trash blunder to about 300 people. When I told the story, I figured that Beverly would receive a little good-natured razzing from her new colleagues. Instead, women from all over the building were calling to offer her clothes, volunteering to take her shopping, wanting to know what sizes she wore, and offering to take up a collection in their departments to help her buy new clothes.

Beverly was a little irritated with me, but I think she was also overwhelmed by the way people had responded to her crisis. Fortunately, Beverly had a sense of humor, and I think she ultimately forgave me for exposing her goof to the world. But she never forgot how people at Southwest responded to a fellow employee in need.

A few weeks later, I happened to wander past Beverly's office late one evening. She was working late, as usual, so I stopped in. The next week happened to include Martin Luther King's birthday. At Southwest, corporate offices did not close to celebrate the day, but employees were free to use one of their so-called floating holidays, which could also be used to celebrate religious holidays or other days of importance. Beverly had a picture of Dr. King in her office, so I knew that she respected this hero of human freedom and would want to honor him appropriately. In making conversation, I mentioned to Beverly that she was, of course, welcome to take the holiday to honor Dr. King.

Beverly smiled and looked at the picture of Dr. King with reverence. "No, I figure that everything he did was so I *could* come to work. I honor his birthday every year by coming to work."

Beverly went on to become head of the People department at Southwest and now works for another great company, Ticketmaster, where she leads their human resources department. This year, she called me on Martin Luther King's birthday to let me know she was thinking of me. She was at home, she said, because Ticketmaster closed its offices to honor Dr. King's birthday. She just wanted me to know that even though she was at home, she was working.

Chapter 32

Fun Can Have a Purpose

Fun is not just about having parties and celebrations, but such things are usually common at places where people enjoy their work. They give people of all levels in the organization a chance to meet, mingle, and get to know each other.

Before Southwest moved into our new headquarters building in 1990, our general offices were located in the dilapidated old East Terminal of Dallas Love Field. It was a fairly bizarre setup. Since the building had once been an airline terminal, it was long and narrow. Our quarters were about 60 feet wide and 1,000 feet long, with a narrow hallway from one end to the other.

But one of the good things about the facility was Howdy's, the little delicatessen right in the midst of the East Terminal. Well, maybe Howdy's wasn't so good at lunch, but after 5:00 it had a superb collection of beers from all over the world—and it was cheap. Needless to say, Howdy's was a popular hangout for Southwest employees after work. And on Fridays, the place really buzzed.

At this point, my office, along with that of my old law partner, Ron Ricks, was right across the narrow hall from Howdy's. The smell of corned beef hung in the air every afternoon. Both Ron and I were accustomed to working late, but on Friday afternoons it was impossible to get any work done after 5:00. The crowd in Howdy's quickly became too boisterous to concentrate on work. So what was I to do? Go have a beer, of course.

The Friday gatherings at Howdy's became a ritual. People from one end of the long hall to the other who hadn't had a chance to see each other all week would embrace (we did a lot of hugging at Southwest) and catch up on the week's events. They would swap stories about funny things that had happened to them that week, catch up on families and friends, and talk about whatever evil plot had been hatched by our competitors. Rank didn't matter. Executives and people who had dirt under their fingernails were drinking together and swapping stories.

After a while, I started to notice that this wasn't just a social event. It was a cultural phenomenon. People didn't just enjoy their work; they enjoyed being with the people they worked with. And, I noticed after a while, work was actually happening at these gatherings. Amid the laughter and swapping of stories, people were also sharing information and ideas. I don't know exactly how many ideas for improving our business were either created or communicated at Howdy's, but it was more than a few.

When it came time to move into our new headquarters building, Howdy's didn't move with us. Our new cafeteria vendor didn't want to serve beer. The Friday gatherings at Howdy's were in danger of extinction. This couldn't happen.

So we decided to preserve the tradition of Friday afternoons at Howdy's. Fortunately our new headquarters building had a beautiful outdoor deck on the third floor, complete with a fantastic view overlooking the entire airport and downtown Dallas. We decided this was a natural. So the General Counsel department became the host for our Friday deck parties.

Everybody in the department pitched in. We would ice down the beer on Friday afternoons, haul it up to the deck at 5:00, and serve it to those who showed up from throughout the company. For years, my executive assistant, Marilyn, was well known at our neighborhood liquor store. She was the personable lady who showed up at lunch once a week and bought about 40 cases of beer. We collected donations from those attending the deck parties to cover expenses. Anything left over either went to charity or helped pay for future employee events. Whenever I spoke to employee groups who wanted to know what I did as General Counsel, I always told them my most important function was supervising the beverage selection for our Friday deck parties.

Another quirky thing we did at Southwest was to celebrate Halloween with a vengeance. Employees at every airport would decorate their ticket counters and gate areas with a theme of their choosing, and come to work in appropriate costumes. Flight attendants would entertain customers by welcoming them aboard in some highly original costumes. Each department in the headquarters would select a theme, and the entire building became home to a holiday festival. Some departments would put on talent shows, displaying the often impressive talent of their departments. Others would do elaborately choreographed musical presentations, frequently involving a parody of recent events in the airline industry. Office areas became haunted houses for a day. Employees' families flooded the building to participate in the festivities, as did outside friends, public officials, and groups of schoolchildren. Not much work got done on Halloween.

I must confess that when I first came to Southwest, I was skeptical that this was a wise allocation of resources. Most of the preparations took place after hours and at lunchtime, but there was no doubt that a lot of working hours were spent preparing for Halloween and on the events of the day itself. Any efficiency expert would have been horrified.

But then one day during a lunchtime planning session for our department's upcoming Halloween show, I noticed the strangest thing. The people in charge of organizing Halloween were not the people who were normally in charge of things. Secretaries were giving orders to their bosses. People who usually gave orders were being told to do the silliest things and were agreeing to do them. One year, I was one of three executives who got roped into performing a rather humiliating skit based on the most outrageous scenes from the movie *The Three Amigos*. Along with our vice president of government affairs and my old law partner, Ron Ricks, and our executive vice president, John Denison (who would later become CEO of ATA Airlines after his retirement from Southwest), we seriously rehearsed and choreographed our skit and apparently gave a memorable performance, of which I am still reminded from time to time. I think the concluding pelvic thrust was one of those horrible images people just couldn't get out of their minds.

Halloween turned the corporate pyramid on its head. Rank meant nothing, and everybody had a chance to assume an unaccustomed role. Rank-and-file workers became bosses, and bosses had to take orders. Halloween wasn't just fun, I finally figured out. It was fun with a purpose. Everybody had an opportunity to learn something—and we had a chance to see some superb leadership talent from people at every level of the company.

Chapter 33

Celebrate Success and Achievement

When people do a good job, they like to be recognized for it. The reward doesn't have to be anything big. For example, Jim Ruppel, who is Southwest Airlines' vice president of customer relations, routinely ran contests to see which employee or team of employees could satisfactorily resolve the most customer issues, receive the most customer compliments, or achieve some other standard of success. The prizes weren't big—maybe a movie ticket or a restaurant gift certificate. But the competition was intense and good-natured. Almost every department had some form of employee recognition program, and they all let employees know their work was meaningful and appreciated.

On a grander scale, we had numerous forms of employee recognition. Every year we held an extravagant awards banquet, where we honored all employees celebrating their 10-, 20-, 25-, or 30-year anniversaries with the company. In addition, each department recognized winners of an annual President's Award. Thousands of employees and spouses came from all over the country to participate.

Several times during the year, we also recognized employees who had been nominated by customers or fellow employees for special recognition with a so-called Winning Spirit Award. We brought the winners and their spouses to our headquarters in Dallas, where they were treated like royalty.

While I was CEO, I always made a special effort to meet with the extraordinary people who had won Winning Spirit Awards because I found the stories of their deeds to be so moving. Several had heroically saved the lives of customers or fellow employees. One airport employee had used his own car to drive an elderly customer from Phoenix to Tucson when she learned her daughter had been in a serious accident and she had no other way to get there. One airport ramp agent had given her winter jacket to a customer who didn't have one. A reservations agent had used her day off to meet an elderly first time flyer at the airport because our employee could tell when she booked the reservation that the customer would have difficulty dealing with the airport. The list went on and on. None of these employees had been told to do these things, nor had they asked permission. They had just done what they thought was the right thing to do—and they had done it without any expectation that they would ever be recognized for their good deeds. The stories always uplifted my spirits and helped me remember why we were successful.

Good people who want to offer legendary customer service can do amazing things. We all seem to work harder and better when we know that our work is valued and our efforts are appreciated. That's a big part of what makes work fun.

Chapter 34

Creating Entrepreneurs

Entrepreneurs are people who start or run businesses with creative ideas. They take risks. They challenge the status quo, and sometimes they change the world.

Entrepreneurs do not just do their jobs. They think like owners. Owners are constantly looking for ways to improve the business, grow revenues, cut costs, enhance customer service, and create competitive advantages.

Classic organizational theory, as generally practiced through most of the twentieth century, involved an emphasis on clearly defined and specialized jobs. This classic structure involved clear boundaries between functions, reinforced by a rigid chain of command. Detailed rules and standard operating procedures governed conduct and decisions. This organizational structure is commonly known as *bureaucracy*.

An organizational bureaucracy does offer certain advantages. Specialization promotes efficiency. Reliance on formal rules and standard operating procedures promotes predictability and consistency. It is easy to see why this organizational structure flourished in an industrial society and why governmental units seeking to administer massive programs with consistency also adopted it.

Bureaucracy has severe limitations, however. It discourages individual thinking and quashes creativity. Rank-and-file employees are simply required to do their jobs with precision. They have no need to understand the mission of the organization, how their jobs fit into the overall picture, or how their individual success is connected to the success of the organization.

From the classic bureaucratic organization's standpoint, it did not particularly matter whether employees felt challenged or fulfilled. It is no wonder that employees came to think of themselves as cogs in a giant wheel, while management came to think of labor as a capital asset that could be depreciated and discarded when no longer useful. This labor-management schism grew so wide in many legacy companies that it continues to threaten their very existence to this day.

Entrepreneurs hate bureaucracy. They generally understand the need for structure and a chain of command, but they can't stand to be told to keep their thinking inside the box. Entrepreneurs think like owners. They are always trying to improve the business because they care about its success.

Twenty-first century organizations live in a world that will tolerate neither the sluggishness of bureaucracy nor the labor-management schism that accompanies it. Modern organizations live in a globally competitive, networked world, where change occurs and information travels instantaneously. Customers demand value and customized service as never before. A competitive world economy ensures that customers will get what they want. A business that does not give customers what they want at a price they are willing to pay will be replaced by a competitor who will.

To succeed in this competitive world, businesses must have the ability to identify the need for change, to implement change, and to adapt to change quickly. Bureaucratic organizations do not change quickly. Businesses that succeed in this kaleidoscopic economy will not be the sluggish, nor those consumed with internal warfare between labor and management. Successful businesses will be filled with people at all levels who share a common vision of success.

A shared vision of success means that employees must think like owners, and managers must think like servant leaders. The ultimate success of any organization, as well as the success of any leader, depends greatly on the commitment employees feel toward the success of their company's mission. Successful and dynamic organizations want employees who think like entrepreneurs.

One of my favorite entrepreneurs at Southwest Airlines was named Dave Spears. Before his retirement, Dave was our long-time director of facilities. At a time when Southwest didn't have much money to spend, Dave was responsible for constructing airport facilities to accommodate the airline's rapid growth. A more conventional company would have never tolerated Dave. He had little formal education, and he wasn't much on paperwork. If you had asked him to prepare a PowerPoint presentation, he would have looked at you like you were from Mars. But Dave was always thinking of new ideas. I considered him a genius, actually. And we gave Dave room to think outside the box.

When we wanted to fly to Nashville and no ticket counter space was available, Dave figured out how to turn a trailer into a ticket counter. When we wanted to beat a competitor into Little Rock, Dave figured out how to build the facilities in ten days. (Such a project usually takes at least three to four months.) When we ran out of gate space in Oakland, Dave figured out how to build a connecting bridge to another terminal so that our operations could flow over into unused gates there. Everywhere we grew, Dave found new challenges, and every time he came up with ideas no conventional thinker would have dreamed of.

One of my first experiences with Dave came in 1986, shortly after I became General Counsel of Southwest. Although Dave technically reported to me, I recognized that he was a lot smarter than I was. As was usually my situation, the people who reported to me knew a lot more about how to do their jobs than I did. This allowed me to perform what is sometimes the most important job of management—getting out of the way.

When Southwest began service to Phoenix in 1982, all modern facilities in the airport terminal had been rented to other airlines. Because none of those airlines was anxious to see Southwest and its notoriously low fares come to town, nobody would make room for or share facilities with the new competitor. So Southwest cast its eyes on an old, abandoned building down the road. It turned out to be the original terminal for Phoenix Sky Harbor Airport, which had been abandoned years earlier by all the other airlines in favor of more modern facilities.

Southwest's properties and facilities team managed to clean the cobwebs out of the old building, but amenities were pretty primitive. Since the old terminal had been built in 1952, it was something of a period piece. After checking in, passengers had to walk outside and board the airplane by climbing up air stairs. Arriving passengers claimed their bags in an outdoor area next to the building. But in 1982, Southwest occupied the old building and started flying. And the passengers came.

By 1986, we were growing in Phoenix and actually wanted to build some indoor facilities from which our Phoenix passengers could board their flights. We thought this would be pretty uptown, even though passengers would still have to take a short outdoor walk to get to the new gates. But we still weren't rolling in money.

Because an airplane's door is about 18 feet off the ground, all modern airports place passenger hold rooms and boarding facilities on the second floor of the terminal building. Jet bridges are designed to connect directly from a two-story structure to an airplane door. But a two-story structure would have been prohibitively expensive for us to build. After all, Southwest was a low fare airline, and it had to keep costs down.

The old one-story terminal in Phoenix was built before modern boarding bridges. In the interest of economy, we wanted to build our new gates as a one-story structure also. But we also wanted to give our passengers the experience of boarding the airplane through an enclosed jet bridge. No existing technology allowed for connecting a one-story building to an airplane door without the use of air stairs. So the job fell to Dave to figure out how we could overcome this dilemma.

Sure enough, Dave knew the solution. We would build a one-story annex to the original terminal, just as planned. To keep passengers out of the weather, we would simply build an upward sloping tunnel ramp from the hold room to the aircraft parking position. This allowed Southwest the economy of a one-story structure while allowing our customers the benefit of weather protected jet bridge boarding.

And Dave figured we could save a bunch more money by installing a fixed bridge resting on a fixed pedestal. This was a lot less expensive than the moving jet bridges used by other airlines, who needed the flexibility of mobile bridges to access their many different aircraft types. Because Southwest operated only one aircraft type, the Boeing 737, we didn't need this expensive piece of equipment. We knew exactly what kind of plane was coming every time, and we could build our facilities accordingly.

In retrospect, it all seems pretty simple and logical. The amazing thing was that nobody had done it before. The key was that Dave wasn't just checking off boxes on a "to do" list. He was using his head.

By the time I got to Phoenix to inspect the project, it was almost done. The airplanes were coming in two days, however, and there was still a lot of work to be done. When I walked into the construction site, I had trouble finding anybody I could recognize. When I finally found Dave, along with our manager (later to become vice president) of properties, Bob Montgomery, they weren't supervising the project. They were working. They were in the midst of hanging speakers from the ceiling, and they were so covered in sawdust and sweat that I didn't even recognize them at first. Unfortunately, I'm a lawyer and not a carpenter, so I wasn't much help to them. About all I could do that was of any use was to take the work crew to dinner.

One final crisis arose in the final days before we could open the new gates. When Dave got the bill for the fancy new electronic signs directing passengers to the proper gates, he went through the roof. The sign company wanted over $20,000. Dave thought that was outrageous, so he sent the signs back and went to Wal-Mart himself, where he found a simple liquid crystal display sign for about $250. It wasn't as fancy, and it required a little more work by our employees to program it for every flight, but nobody seemed to mind. Our customers knew we were saving money to keep their fares low. And our employees knew the money we saved was going into their profitsharing accounts.

Incidentally, when I saw Dave recently, he was enjoying his retirement and working on his latest invention— air conditioning his golf cart by flowing air through his beer cooler. Why didn't I think of that?

Chapter 35

Encourage Unconventional Thinking

"Everything that can be invented has been invented."
—Charles H. Duell, Commissioner
of the U.S. Office of Patents, 1899

Prepare yourself for a shock: Not everything has already been invented. Not every great idea has already occurred. Not every valuable innovation has already been implemented. And nobody knows everything there is to know.

The world advances through change and new ideas. The twenty-first century economy is changing at breakneck speed due to a combination of macroeconomic forces, including:

- Profound technological changes, touching every business
- Instantaneous worldwide communication and information gathering capability

- Deregulation and privatization of previously regulated industries, including telecommunications, banking, trucking, and airlines
- A worldwide movement toward a competitive, free enterprise business model
- Consumer empowerment, which is driven by all the previous factors

The world is becoming more globally competitive. Businesses are becoming leaner and more efficient. Customers are demanding better quality at a lower price. Those who stand still will be overtaken and will ultimately perish.

In the classic bureaucratic business model, employees were just required to "do their jobs." The task of thinking, visioning, and innovating was entrusted to a separate department. After due deliberation, the Research and Development department might decide to add tail fins next year, more chrome the following year, and optional seat belts some time in the future, for example. Companies that still think that way today are being left behind.

Today's consumer-driven world does not allow such a structured or sluggish approach to change. Long-term planning is certainly still appropriate and necessary, especially with respect to financial planning and projects requiring a long lead time. At the same time, long-term planning must be undertaken with the knowledge that the world will change continuously as we go along.

How will we know when to change and how? Will the R&D department tell us? Perhaps, but it is just as likely our employees and customers will tell us first, if we just listen.

Unconventional thinking by employees can be trying. Leaders may occasionally feel uncomfortable and even threatened by what they hear. If you listen, you will probably encounter many of the same ideas you have heard before. Sometimes, for reasons not obvious to employees, these ideas simply do not fit your company's business model. Frequently, the uncertain benefits of a promising idea simply do not justify the costs.

And dealing with unconventional thinking is time consuming. You must give new ideas a fair hearing and let employees know their thinking is valued and appreciated, even if their ideas are not accepted.

Every once in a while, however, an employee will tell you something that lights up your eyes. For example, if you are in the airline industry, an employee might tell you exactly how you could use existing technology to eliminate the need for paper tickets, saving millions of dollars a year. This happened to me.

In 1994, Southwest Airlines faced a crisis that would define the future of the company. At the time, all airlines sold a majority of their tickets through travel agencies. Most airlines sold about 90 percent of their tickets that way. Southwest sold less—about 60 percent—because many of our customers simply preferred to call us directly. But travel agency sales still accounted for a majority of our business.

Virtually all travel agents used computer reservation systems to book travel and print tickets. These systems were owned and controlled by our larger competitors—primarily American, United, Delta, Northwest, TWA, US Air, and Continental. Smaller airlines, such as Southwest, were expected to pay the owners of the computer reservation systems in order for travel agents to issue the smaller airlines' tickets. Most smaller airlines reluctantly agreed to pay the price, feeling it was their only way to gain access to the market.

At Southwest, we had a different view. We viewed the computer reservation system fees as an unnecessary expense. It was simply a scheme to divert revenue from our bottom line to the bottom lines of our competitors—simply because they had the market power to demand it.

As the competitive threat from Southwest's low fares began to spread, our larger competitors decided it was time to put an end to the matter once and for all. They launched a two-pronged attack.

First, several larger airlines started their own low fare "airline within an airline," with the express purpose of preventing further growth by, or destroying, Southwest Airlines. United Shuttle tried to retake California for United; Continental Lite popped up in the Southeast; US Air and Delta had their own brands. All of these "airlines within airlines" lost massive amounts of money, and all were ultimately dismantled when it became clear how much this folly was costing the big airlines.

The second prong of the predatory attack involved the computer reservation systems that the large airlines owned. Despite the fact that Southwest had historically refused to pay, all the systems nonetheless allowed our tickets to be printed—because customers and travel agents demanded it. But now the long knives came out. Virtually simultaneously, our competitors announced that they were locking Southwest out. Travel agents would no longer be able to print tickets on Southwest. Suddenly, Southwest faced the threat that we would be cut off from a huge portion of our customers—and our revenue.

It was another seemingly insoluble conundrum. If we refused to pay, we knew that we could lose massive amounts of revenue, threatening our financial viability. But if we paid, we knew that it would begin a continuous transfer of wealth from Southwest to our competitors, as we would be required to pay them every time we sold a ticket. In studying the issue, we noticed that every independent airline that had agreed to the wealth transfer had ultimately gone out of business or been acquired by one of the big airlines: Midway, Ozark, Piedmont, Frontier, Western, PSA, Air California—all proud names in the history of aviation that no longer existed. We didn't want Southwest to join the list.

So we made our decision. In essence, we defiantly said to our competitors, "Millions for defense, but not one cent for tribute." We wouldn't pay.

Gulp. That was brave. What do we do now?

Faced with the imminent loss of a huge portion of our business, we tried a number of stopgap measures. If travel agents would sell our tickets, we would send the tickets to them by mail. If the travel agent or customer needed the ticket sooner, we would send it by Federal Express for overnight delivery. We experimented with putting some of our own computers and ticket printers in travel agents' offices. All the solutions were expensive, costing us more money than if we had just caved in and paid the fees our competitors demanded. And none of the solutions really satisfied all our customers. We were in a real bind.

And then one of our employees, named Mike Golden, stopped me in the hall and pulled me into an empty office. Mike headed a small department in our company called technical services. They mostly fixed broken computers and helped install technical equipment when we opened service to a new airport. They were a hard working, highly dedicated group who exemplified the culture of Southwest Airlines. But their area of work did not really involve marketing decisions or software development. Because I was General Counsel at the time, these areas were well outside my realm of responsibility as well.

I knew Mike well. He was another one of the geniuses whom I theoretically supervised but knew to be a lot smarter than I was. Once we were out of the public hallway, Mike started talking to me in a low but excited voice. I didn't understand much of the technical things he was telling me, but when he got to the punch line, my eyes lit up. His team had figured out how we could implement *ticketless* travel, using our existing equipment and technology. It would take some relatively simple software adjustments and could be accomplished within a few weeks.

This was the answer to a prayer. Ticketless travel would allow travel agents to sell seats on Southwest without having to use ticket printers. Travel agents could simply book seats over the telephone and take a credit card number. They could do this without using our competitors' systems.

We knew ticketless travel could work. When we acquired Morris Air at the end of 1993, Morris had already developed its own ticketless system, which had been well received by customers. I had come to know and respect David Neeleman, who was the president of Morris, and David told us that ticketless travel had worked great at Morris. (David would later start JetBlue Airlines.) With a ticketless system, travel agents would be liberated from the ticket printers owned by our competitors' computer reservation systems and would once again be able to sell seats on Southwest with relative ease. But Morris was much smaller than Southwest, and our computer systems were not compatible.

The problem was time. Adapting the Morris system to our needs or developing our own ticketless system was projected to take months or years, with no assurance of success. Now Mike Golden was telling me we could use our existing technology and hardware to go ticketless in a matter of weeks instead of months or years. It was a miracle.

Mike and I quickly split up assignments. Mike would talk to our executive vice president, John Denison. John was very smart and would understand the technical issues I couldn't. He also supervised the systems department, which would be necessary to implement the software changes that Mike's idea would require. Incidentally, after John retired from Southwest a few years later, he became the chairman and CEO of ATA Airlines, which was in bankruptcy at the time. Against seemingly insurmountable obstacles, he saved ATA and brought it out of bankruptcy as an independent airline. As I said, he was very smart. On this occasion, he was smart enough to understand Mike's ideas, and he personally spearheaded the ticketless developmental program.

My job was to talk to Herb Kelleher, our chairman and CEO at the time, who would need to authorize the development effort. I don't think Herb initially understood many more of the technical details than I did, but he quickly saw the business potential.

Within weeks, Southwest became the first major airline in the world (Morris was far too small to be classified as a "major" airline according to government standards) to implement ticketless travel. The day was saved. After appropriate testing, ticketless travel was introduced nationwide by Southwest Airlines in January 1995.

Because we had developed ticketless travel, Southwest was able to revolutionize the airline industry once again in 1996, when it became the first major airline to offer seats for sale through its own Internet site. Internet sales would not have been feasible at the time without ticketless travel. Once again, the entire project was conceived, developed, and implemented internally by rank-and-file employees who simply had the courage and the vision to think unconventionally.

By listening to our employees, we beat the competition by several years in these endeavors and saved hundreds of millions of dollars in distribution costs over the next decade.

By the way, Mike Golden, the guy who dared to think outside the box, was recently asked to become the chief technology officer of the United States Transportation Security Administration, where he has been tasked with overhauling and modernizing the entire technological foundation for our nation's aviation security. I have great confidence that our nation will benefit tremendously from his creative thinking.

Chapter 36

Suggestion Boxes

Many companies seek to promote employee involvement with suggestion boxes. Suggestion boxes are not necessarily a bad idea, although we never had one at Southwest Airlines.

Suggestion boxes tend to be a bit sterile, reflecting the more formal structure of classic bureaucratic organizations. They can reinforce a culture in which the response of frontline supervisors to new ideas is "Put it in the suggestion box." They can become a black hole from which employee suggestions receive no more of a response than a rubber stamp, "Idea Rejected."

To be useful, suggestion boxes require constant attention by management. Every suggestion requires a thoughtful and prompt reply, complete with an explanation of the reasoning behind the response. Otherwise, employees will understand that their ideas are not taken seriously, and the suggestion box will probably soon be filled with rather unkind "suggestions" about what the company can do with its box. Even if done well, however, the process lacks spontaneous interactivity.

The absence of a suggestion box need not convey a message that management is disinterested in employee ideas. Rather, it can convey a message that any employee is encouraged to contribute ideas at any time, to any level of management. Of course, that depends on the entire culture of the organization and on leaders who are truly open to new ideas.

In a truly open environment where unconventional thinking is encouraged, frontline leaders will not respond to ideas by simply saying, "Put it in the suggestion box." Rather, they will personally engage the employee in a thoughtful exchange as to why the idea might or might not work. The supervisor might say, "You know, we actually tried that a couple of years ago, and here's what happened." Or "We've looked at that idea several times. It would save some money, but we just don't think it would fit with the overall experience we want to give our customers." Or "That's an interesting idea. Let me look into it and get back to you."

Of course, the latter response requires a leader who actually follows up with further investigation and a subsequent report back to the employee. That's servant leadership.

Chapter 37

Many Roads Lead to the Promised Land

A lot of companies believe in measuring success. "Metrics" seem to be the order of the day. "If you can't measure it, you can't manage it," I once heard a great business leader say. Measuring things has become so pervasive that I sometimes wonder whether they teach anything in business schools anymore except how to make bar charts, line graphs, and pie charts for PowerPoint presentations.

In my perhaps outmoded view, this manic stampede toward measuring everything poses a danger to the success of many organizations. The risk is that we are not measuring the right things. The risk is that we are focusing excessively on the discrete steps of a process rather than on the right outcomes. Process is revered over results.

Excessive focus on measuring each step in a process creates a silo mentality. In other words, employees come to focus only on what happens in their silo. A silo is a tall, cylindrical structure used to store grain or missiles. It is shut off from the rest of the world. If employees come to realize that they are measured only by what happens in their silo, then that is what they will focus on. They will not care about or understand the links between their jobs and the jobs performed by their colleagues in other functions. Consequently, when they are forced to exercise judgment in balancing the relative importance of conflicting goals, they are totally unprepared to do so.

Don't get me wrong. I am certainly not opposed to measuring success. We just need to measure the right things, and the right things are usually pretty simple. When measurements focus on process rather than outcomes, they threaten to undermine the teamwork that goes into the successful performance of the ultimate mission.

In defining the right outcomes, I think it is easiest to start with the big things. In the free enterprise system, the most basic measure of success by a private business is profitability—not just one quarter or one year of profits, but a sustainable basis for consistent and growing profits. This is the goal of any business. This is the guiding light from which all subsidiary goals must flow. This is why it is important for all people of an organization to understand and embrace the importance of their company's profitability as an ultimate goal of everything they do.

Every company has a strategy to achieve sustained profitability. This is the road map to the ultimate goal, which employees and managers also need to understand. For example, in a customer service business such as the airline industry, customer satisfaction must be a major part of the business strategy. Unhappy customers may not come back, or at least will defect at the first opportunity.

Safety, of course, will be a major part of the business strategy for an airline. An airline with a bad safety record will not attract many paying passengers, and it probably will not even be allowed to fly by regulatory authorities. Efficiency and operational integrity must be major parts of the strategy. Inefficient or poorly operated airlines do not make money.

These are major goals. On time performance, for example, is a subsidiary part of the overriding goals of customer satisfaction, efficiency, and safety. It is not uncommon for airline employees to be forced to make decisions that involve conflicting goals. In these situations, they must be prepared to exercise good judgment. They must understand which goals are most important and how they fit together. For example, the desire to depart on time always ranks below a true safety issue.

But the decision to operate on time frequently involves the exercise of judgment. If it is time to close the door and a customer is running late, what do you do? Companies that have a silo mentality may have inflexible rules. It is impossible to write a policy manual covering every conceivable situation, however. The facts of every situation are always different. If you have employees who understand the true goals of your company, they can exercise their judgment to make good decisions, taking into account all the facts and circumstances.

If a customer is just checking bags at the ticket counter and the plane is about to push back, for example, you probably won't hold the plane. On the other hand, if a customer is running toward the gate and is 15 seconds away, you probably will. Those are pretty simple.

But what if you have connecting passengers on an incoming flight who will be stranded overnight in the connecting city if you don't hold the flight? Or what if the people just checking bags at the ticket counter are firefighters who have just volunteered to go fight a major forest fire in New Mexico? This one really happened. Fortunately, our employees exercised their judgment and decided to take a 15-minute delay so the firefighters could get to the gate. How did the delayed passengers respond? When the plane landed at its destination, all the passengers stayed in their seats to let the courageous firefighters get off first and gave them a hearty round of applause as they departed. The on time performance for that plane suffered that day, but everybody felt pretty good about it.

Our employees not only had good judgment; they felt empowered to use it. They knew how important on time performance is. They also knew that we had one overriding plea to all our people—when in doubt, *just do the right thing*. It may be a somewhat subjective standard, but it usually led to good results. It required our people to use their heads. It required them to understand what our company was about. Sometimes it drove them to make decisions from the heart.

I recall one snowy night in the Midwest. It was the night before Thanksgiving. When one of our planes landed in Chicago, it had one more flight scheduled for that evening, to Detroit. In Detroit, the plane would sit in the snow and the crew would seek the warmth of a hotel room until Thanksgiving morning.

In Chicago, all the Chicago-bound passengers got off—all except for one young girl who was confused about where she was. The plane reloaded and took off for Detroit with the young girl still on board. When it arrived, all the Detroit-bound passengers got off—except for the young girl, whose family was now in a panic in Chicago wondering where their daughter was.

It was our mistake, no doubt about it. And when the captain figured out what had happened, he knew what he was going to do about it. He didn't ask for permission; he just did it. He asked his flight crew to climb back on the airplane and told the Detroit station to call Chicago to let the girl's parents know their daughter was coming. I don't know how much money that unscheduled round trip between Detroit and Chicago cost us that night, but I sure was proud when I heard the story. Once again, our people just did the right thing.

I sometimes worry that today's technology will lead to the demise of human judgment. Some thoughtful observers, such as MIT Professor of Information Technologies Tom Malone, have prophesied that "these technologies now make it possible for many more people, even in huge organizations, to have the information they need to make decisions for themselves, instead of just following orders from above."

I hope Tom Malone is right, but I fear that we must guard against the opposite result. I fear that the rapidity of modern communication will encourage megalomaniac managers to gather even more meaningless data and try to micromanage every situation, in the name of consistency and uniformity. This is not progress. It is a reversion to the assembly line mentality of a bygone era when people just did their jobs and did what they were told.

If we learned anything from the failure of centrally planned economies, it should be that many roads lead to the Promised Land. There is frequently more than one way to accomplish a mission, and the same decision does not fit every situation.

Empowering frontline employees to exercise judgment and make decisions has its risks. Sometimes they will make bad decisions and you will have to kick their butts before you send them out to make more decisions. But if they are properly empowered, trained, and motivated, and if they think like owners, they will usually make good decisions. If given the opportunity, they will usually do the right things. And when they do, they will give your organization that secret sauce that others don't have.

Chapter 38

Define the Right Goals and Give People Room to Succeed

The first job of any leader is to define the real goals his or her team is trying to accomplish—the *real* goals, not the artificial ones. The best customer service companies distinguish themselves by defining the right goals for their people.

For example, if you work at a technical support help desk, your group may have a benchmark as to how many calls you would like to handle in an hour or a day. That benchmark is, no doubt, a useful tool to help manage the workflow, but it is not *the* goal. The goal is to help your customers by solving their problems. What is the standard of success by which employees are judged? Are they judged by how many calls they handled or by how many customers they satisfied?

Dell computers revolutionized the personal computer industry with reliable, inexpensive computers, which are sold directly to customers. The company, founded by Michael Dell in his dorm room at The University of Texas in the 1980s, became so successful that it drove less efficient, higher cost competitors entirely out of the PC business. Dell's market share soared. Customers also loved the company's commitment to service after the sale. Dell's reputation for customer service became legendary, and the company was the envy of the industry—a low cost company known for its customer service.

As inevitably happens in a free market economy, inefficient competitors were driven from the marketplace but were replaced by others who figured out how to match Dell's low cost structure. Suddenly, Dell was no longer alone in offering high quality computers at a low cost. Indeed, by the twenty-first century, the prices of Dell computers were often higher than those of good quality competitors.

Dell responded by trying to cut costs even more. It shifted call centers to India and other lower cost locations. It began using more temporary workers, who are a lot less expensive than full-time employees. The people helping Dell's customers were, no doubt, plenty intelligent and technically competent. But they didn't necessarily understand the expectations of Dell's customers. Apparently, Dell executives didn't understand those expectations either.

Customers noticed the changes. Their problems weren't being solved. They had to call back repeatedly with the same problems.

Dell's computers were still fine, but the after-sale service was not. Dell's reputation as a customer service company plummeted almost overnight. And the company felt the impact. According to *Fortune* magazine,

Dell's internal "likely to repurchase" score among existing customers was falling fast. Dell's legendary bond with its historically loyal customers was crumbling.

Founder Michael Dell told *Fortune* magazine what had happened and what he was doing about it. Managers had been evaluating call center employees primarily based on how long they stayed on the phone with each customer. Predictably enough, employees responded to the standard of success by which they were being measured. Customers' problems weren't being solved; customers were just being handled as expeditiously as possible. When problems weren't solved with the first call, customers had to call back again and again. This not only produced unhappy customers; it consumed valuable resources.

Dell was smart enough to recognize the problem. It changed the way it evaluated its employees and began to base evaluations on how well customers' problems were solved on the first call. Once again, employees responded to the standard of success by which they were measured. Customers' problems began to be solved with much more regularity. Fewer angry customers had to call back a second or third time with the same problem.

Within weeks, Dell could see the impact. Internal measures of customer satisfaction improved. The number of existing customers saying they were likely to repurchase Dell products in the future went up, returning to prior levels.

Employee productivity likewise improved. Because customer problems were being solved on the first call, Dell had two million fewer calls than it had planned in the second quarter of 2006. With fewer calls, the average hold time for callers was cut by 50 percent.

Michael Dell summed up his take on the entire experience in *Fortune* magazine:

> We were doing some things that were just plain wrong. The team was managing cost instead of managing service and quality. It's totally the wrong answer. Stop managing for cost. Manage for a great experience.

Michael Dell performed the role of a leader. He defined the proper goals. When he saw that some people were pursuing the wrong goals, or had the priority of their goals out of order, he stepped in and clarified the organization's focus. Then he gave his people room to succeed.

Chapter 39

The Two-Minute Drill

If you have ever watched an American football game, you are probably familiar with what is called the two-minute drill. Time is running out. The team that is behind is trying to drive the ball down the field to score while using as little of the clock as possible. Many fans consider this to be the most exciting part of the game because it is so extemporaneous and unpredictable.

There are several ways to stop the clock in football. A team can call a time out, but it has only a limited number and doesn't want to waste them. A player can run out of bounds. The quarterback can throw an incomplete pass, either intentionally or not. Every play involves strategic decisions. If the clock is running, there is no time for a huddle. Every player must know exactly what to do. Players must know what play will be run. Once a player gets the ball, he must frequently make a split second decision. Should he go out of bounds to stop the clock, or cut up the field in hopes of making a big gain? If he stays in bounds, he may cost his team a valuable time out. But if he goes out of bounds, he may miss the chance to gain critical yardage. Does his team have a time out left? Can he afford the risk?

Every team practices the two-minute drill, but some run it better than others. This is where preparation and good coaching show.

The final seconds of a tight basketball game can be even more fascinating to watch, especially if you enjoy watching leadership styles. The last few seconds of a close game often involve critical decisions of strategy. Should the team with the ball shoot for a two-point shot or a three-point basket? What play should they run? Who should take the shot? Should the team on defense commit a foul before a shot can be gotten off? If so, who should they foul? What kind of defense should they play? Should they press in the back court or play half-court defense?

The majority of coaches, including most who coach professional players in the NBA, routinely call a time out in this situation—frequently stopping play after every change of possession. The coach will call his team together and lay out the strategy, diagramming the play on a chalkboard and telling every player exactly what to do. Sometimes the coach's strategy works; sometimes it doesn't.

A few years ago, I noticed that a few coaches didn't always do this. And they tended to be some of the best coaches with the longest histories of success, like Mike Krzyzewski, Bobby Knight, and Pat Summitt. Sometimes at a critical point in the game when most coaches would call a time out and start coaching, these coaches would just fold their arms and watch their players play.

And their players seemed to know exactly what to do. In fact, they would frequently take the other team by complete surprise. The other team would often relax for a split second, thinking that a time out would surely be called. By the time they realized their opponents were taking the ball down the court for a final shot, it was too late to react.

After I watched this happen a few times, I finally realized what was going on. These coaches didn't have to coach during the last few seconds of the game because they had already done it. They had prepared their players for this situation so well that the players didn't need to be told what to do. The players just had to use their heads to react to the situation and do what they were prepared to do. Just as important, the coach trusted them to do it. The coach made a strategic decision, betting that his or her players were better prepared to handle an extemporaneous situation than the players on the other team.

Coaching is like that, in the business world as in sports. A lot of leaders want to control the strategy for handling every situation. If they could, they would call a time out before every critical decision, draw a diagram, and tell everybody exactly what to do. In a sense, this is natural because the leader probably achieved his or her position by being very good at what he or she does. It is natural for such a leader to want to make sure everything goes perfectly.

But the reality of a large organization is that, unlike in basketball, a CEO, a vice president, or even a frontline supervisor simply will not be around every time an employee must make a critical decision.

Watch any organization for a while, and you can see what kind of culture it has. Are frontline leaders and employees expected to use their heads and make the right decisions, or are they simply expected to know the rules and follow them? Do leaders trust people to make decisions when they face extraordinary situations, or are people afraid to make decisions for fear of violating some policy manual? The answer will tell you a lot about the leaders, and about the organization itself. Do they have confidence that they have picked the right people to be on their team? Are they confident that they have given their people the training and leadership necessary to use their judgment in a critical situation?

I was once asked to define leadership. Because I was in a hurry, rushing from one meeting to another, I quickly wrote down an answer. Ironically, even with years of reflection, I haven't been able to improve on it. I wrote:

> Leadership is defining and communicating the mission; providing guidance as to how it might be accomplished; equipping people with the proper tools (information, training, etc.); motivating and inspiring through selfless dedication and respect for others; providing both positive and negative feedback, including recognition for achievement; and, ultimately, getting out of the way and giving people the ability and authority to accomplish the mission, with the full confidence they will be supported.

In business, as in sports, the two-minute drill is where you get the reward for giving employees the tools to make good decisions. The way people deal with those extemporaneous and unpredictable situations distinguishes a dynamic, customer service–driven company that can compete in the twenty-first century. Staid, by-the-book organizations will likely be left behind. This is where good coaching pays off.

Chapter 40

Give People Something to Believe In—Define a Grand Mission

People want to be part of something meaningful. They want to feel pride in what they do and to be respected for it by their friends, family, and community. They want to be part of something bigger than themselves. Most people have a yearning to feel that they have somehow made the world better or done something to improve other people's lives. Too many people are forced to leave these yearnings at home when they go to work. They see no meaning in their jobs and feel no real gratification when their day is done. This is a tragedy, for both the employee and the employer.

A job is about performing certain functions. It is about showing up on time and going home when your shift is over. It is what people do to earn a paycheck. It requires no emotional engagement and usually does not require much creativity, innovation, or thinking outside the box. Most workers have jobs.

A mission, on the other hand, requires a determined effort to accomplish a goal. People who are on a mission feel a passion for what they are doing and are driven to achieve their goal. At Southwest, we wanted our employees to feel they were on a mission.

Every company has a mission statement. How many employees know it by heart? Probably about as many as can recite the *Iliad* in Greek. At Southwest Airlines, we had a very eloquent mission statement, which most employees had at least read. It said:

> The mission of Southwest Airlines is dedication to the highest quality of Customer Service delivered with a sense of warmth, friendliness, individual pride, and Company Spirit.
>
> We are committed to provide our Employees a stable work environment with equal opportunity for learning and personal growth. Creativity and innovation are encouraged for improving the effectiveness of Southwest Airlines. Above all, Employees will be provided the same concern, respect, and caring attitude within the organization that they are expected to share externally with every Southwest Customer.

In Southwest's case, the mission statement really did more to define the culture we sought to build in our company than to define a business strategy. In fact, it didn't even mention what business we were in. So we still needed to define our business goals. For this, we frequently communicated to employees the same messages we sought to communicate to our customers. In the early days of flying intrastate routes in Texas, Southwest became known as "the love airline." The heart became the airline's unofficial logo, the stock ticker symbol of LUV was adopted, and, of course, the airline's home was Dallas Love Field. The message was broadcast to the world with the memorable slogan, "We're spreading love all over Texas," complete with a catchy musical jingle that had people all over the state humming the tune. The internal message was as powerful as the external message: We're not just flying planes; we're spreading love. (It was, after all, the 1970s.)

In later years, as Southwest expanded its reach from one coast to the other, the airline adopted a new message: "We're giving America the freedom to fly." Again, the message was supported with a catchy musical jingle, which was widely advertised throughout the country. To customers, the slogan conveyed our basic business strategy—low fares, frequent flights, and great customer service. Internally, the message was just as powerful: We're not just flying airplanes; we're providing an important societal benefit. We're making travel affordable for people who couldn't afford to fly before. We're allowing grandmothers to attend graduations and families to take vacations. We're allowing businesspeople to conduct the commercial affairs of the nation. We are contributing to the freedom of Americans. We've democratized the skies. We're giving America the freedom to fly.

This is a grand mission. It's not just about making money or punching a time clock. It's about something meaningful, something that benefits our nation and its people, and something that will leave a lasting imprint on people's lives. It is a mission that inspires pride, passion, and a feeling of ownership. It is a mission that allows people to go home, look in the mirror, and say, "I did something meaningful today." It is a mission worth fighting for. This is a grand mission.

Chapter 41

Create a Culture in Which People Want to Do the Right Things

We live in an era of enhanced public attention to issues of corporate ethics. In the wake of Enron and other well-publicized corporate scandals, it seems that anybody with the power to make a new rule on the subject feels obligated to do so. Congress has passed the Sarbanes-Oxley Act, imposing a multitude of new rules concerning matters of corporate governance and financial reporting. The Financial Accounting Standards Board has revised accounting rules to discourage the granting of employee stock options in the aftermath of perceived abuses by top executives of some companies. Almost every state, as well as the federal government, has now passed laws to protect so-called "whistleblowers." Corporate CEOs and chief financial officers are now required to certify that they have made diligent inquiry to ensure the accuracy of their financial statements. The list goes on.

At Southwest Airlines, of course, we complied with all the corporate governance requirements of federal law, state law, and the New York Stock Exchange. We made diligent inquiry to ensure the accuracy of our financial statements—although I never had any doubt of our duty to do so even before Sarbanes-Oxley. We adopted formal written policies on such things as protection of whistleblowers and the preapproval of audit services, and we adopted a formal code of ethics governing all employees.

Personally, however, I am not sure these written policies really represented an advance from our traditional values of just telling our people to do the right thing, follow the Golden Rule, and use the sense God gave a goose.

To be sure, I was honored during my tenure as CEO to see Southwest Airlines named one of America's "100 Best Corporate Citizens" in *Business Ethics* magazine, to be included in *Global Finance* magazine's list of "World's Most Socially Responsible Companies," and to be named the most admired airline and one of the three most admired companies in America by *Fortune* magazine. I do not believe, however, that these distinctions were earned because of our written policies and procedures governing fundamental issues of integrity.

While I might not normally look to a philosophy professor for business advice, I was struck by some words I read a while back that were written by Professor Paul Woodruff. Professor Woodruff, who serves as the dean of undergraduate studies at The University of Texas at Austin, specializes in the study of ancient philosophy and ethics. But his words were aimed at contemporary issues of corporate ethics when he said:

> Modern ethical theory is mainly about rules.... Rules don't help because (a) they always seem to admit

exceptions, and because (b) they don't connect with human motivation. The trouble with rules is that we are often unsure where to apply them, and even when we are sure, they are not sexy.

Rules do not stop sleaze. Anyone with brains and a business degree can work out a way to make good rules serve a sleazy cause. Good rules are no use without good people to apply them at all levels.

In other words, if we expect people to consistently do the right things, they must *want* to do those things. As Professor Woodruff says, virtue must become a habit and a motivational force.

People who live in a culture in which virtue is expected and rewarded are likely to *want* to do the right things. People adapt to the cultures in which they live. People learn from their cultures what kind of conduct is expected and rewarded. In a culture in which people are rewarded for cheating, people will assume this is the expected behavior. But in a culture in which people are rewarded for honesty, good deeds, and caring for each other, they will recognize these as virtues. And they will *want* to do those things.

Every organization has its own culture. In fact, I think every work location and every shift within a larger organization takes on a culture of its own. People coming into the culture are expected to conform, whether it is a culture of virtue or a culture of iniquity.

Shaping the culture of any group is the unique role of a leader, at any level. It doesn't matter whether the leader is a CEO, a shift supervisor, or simply a frontline employee who is respected by peers. Remember, we are all leaders in some way. The example of our behavior is seen and followed by others. And we are all responsible for the lessons taught by our words and deeds. Great organizations have great leaders at all levels.

Leaders shape the cultures of their groups. If a leader lies to others, he must expect them to lie to him. If a leader expects employees to cheat customers or shareholders, he must expect them to cheat the company as well.

Virtues are not complicated. Most of us learned them from our parents and other role models when we were young. Tell the truth. Don't cheat or steal. Treat other people the way you would like to be treated. As Jon Huntsman says in his book *Winners Never Cheat*:

> The principles we learned as children were simple and fair. They remain simple and fair. With moral compasses programmed in the sandboxes of long ago, we can navigate career courses with values that guarantee successful lives, a path that is good for one's mental and moral well-being, not to mention long-term material success.

Great leaders will create cultures in which virtue and honesty are expected and rewarded. In such a culture, most people will do the right things because they *want* to do those things, not just because somebody made a rule.

As observed by Professor Woodruff, "Virtues call for leadership. Leadership is inherently ethical."

Chapter 42

It's a Family Affair

When I agreed to serve on the board of directors of Texas Roadhouse restaurants, the founder of the company, Kent Taylor, flatly told me that Southwest Airlines was his company's role model. I declined to serve on any other boards while I was CEO at Southwest, but after retiring from that job, I thought it would be fascinating to learn how the principles of Southwest Airlines might be applied to a company in an entirely different line of business. Of all the companies I had encountered who said that Southwest was their role model, I thought that Texas Roadhouse had done as good a job as any company I knew of.

The extraordinary thing that Texas Roadhouse did, in my opinion, was to distinguish between *principles* and *tactics*. They used the principles of Southwest but created unique tactics, which they applied to the restaurant business.

For example, most Texas Roadhouse restaurants do not open for lunch except on weekends. This seemed illogical to me. In the airline industry, one of our goals was to keep our planes flying as much as possible. Those are expensive assets to be sitting around. Why would a restaurant choose to let its building and equipment sit idle at lunch?

The reason, I was told by Steve Ortiz, the chief operating officer, had to do with employees' quality of life. Restaurant employees prefer having a single work shift, I was told, and by doing this, we could have happier and better employees.

Okay, I confess I was a little skeptical about this explanation. It sounded too much like something you would say for public relations purposes. I kept digging, trying to find if there were some other reasons, but I couldn't find one.

The truth of the explanation didn't really hit me until some time later, when my wife and I were sharing a car ride with one of our new restaurant managers and his wife. We were on our way from the Calgary airport to Banff, Canada, where Texas Roadhouse was holding its annual managing partner conference. Every year the company holds a four-day conference for all of its restaurant managers and their spouses, along with other key personnel, their spouses, and vendors. The event combines serious business updates with hard work, motivational discussions, award presentations, and world-class entertainment. Managers from almost all the 250 or so restaurants attend, along with their spouses, and it is always a memorable and motivational event.

On this occasion, the new manager was telling me how happy he was to be with Texas Roadhouse. We had hired him away from another restaurant, where he had built a successful track record. He told me he enjoyed Texas Roadhouse a lot more. The people really seemed to know what they were doing, and it seemed like a lot more fun.

And then his wife started to tell me how *really* happy she was. She told me how hard her husband's previous job had been on their family life.

Restaurant managers frequently try to be on the premises during every meal rush and certainly want to be visible for every employee on every shift. The new manager's wife explained to me how her husband's previous restaurant was open for lunch and dinner, meaning that he'd frequently had to be there at 10:00 in the morning and usually hadn't gotten home until late at night. He'd had two meal rushes to oversee and two shifts of employees to lead. On days when he hadn't worked both shifts, his hours had been unpredictable because he had been on call all day for any kind of crisis. All of this made it very difficult to plan a family life.

It suddenly hit me that what Steve Ortiz had told me wasn't PR at all; it was a brilliant tactic for attracting the best managers and the best employees. I learned that one of the things a lot of restaurant employees hate about their job is the shifting hours. At Texas Roadhouse, employees love having a predictable shift. They don't have to work a day shift on Monday, a night shift on Tuesday, and so forth. Servers also love working the dinner shift, where tips are usually better than at lunch. A lot of employees are college students, or have other obligations during the day, and like the evening hours.

And, of course, managers can be on site most of the time without neglecting their families.

A lot of businesses do not have the luxury of limiting their operating hours to one shift. In the airline industry, for example, we were basically a 24-hour, seven-day-a-week operation. Inevitably, some employees had to work odd hours and holidays. Flight crews had to be on the road and away from their families three or four days a week. All of this had to be hard on family lives. A lot of other businesses face the same issues.

Many dedicated employees who think like owners and want to be part of a company's grand mission also have families to whom they feel obligations. This can either create conflict or create a support system.

I always felt the best approach was to include employees' families in our company family. For example, we specifically invited employees to bring their family members to our annual Message to the Field, where employees received an update on the company's business. We had a lot of company parties, celebrations, and special events where spouses were warmly welcomed. Employees' spouses regularly received birthday greetings. New babies were greeted with showers and gifts. We usually tried to send important company information to employees' homes, where it was more likely to be shared with family members.

In recent years, we took all of this to a new level with our pilot training classes. We started to invite the spouses of our new pilots to join us for a one-week orientation in Dallas while the new pilots were in their initial training classes. This was a great opportunity to welcome entire families into the company and to help them share the same passion for our mission that we wanted our employees to feel.

It is a lot easier for a person to make the extraordinary commitment to a company's success if that person's family shares the vision. It always made me feel good to see an employee's child beam with pride when saying, "My mom or dad works for Southwest Airlines."

From personal experience, I can tell you how important it is to have a family that shares your passion for your work. My wife, Pat, was always a wonderful support. She got to know as many Southwest employees as she could and always made a special effort to make their spouses feel welcome. When I was General Counsel, if an employee in our department got married or had a baby, Pat would pick out and wrap the gift that we sent. Since she knew most of our people personally, she usually tried to personalize the gift. When I was CEO, she attended every party and Message to the Field with me, again making a special effort to meet employees and make their families feel welcome.

At the same time, she was a devout guardian of our family values. Inevitably, I missed some of the special moments in our children's lives. But, thanks largely to Pat, I made a lot of them, too. I sometimes groused about her making me be there when I could have been doing something at work, but I'm glad she did. Looking back, I wouldn't have missed those moments for anything.

I think my son, James, and daughter, Jennifer, loved Southwest Airlines almost as much as I did. When he was about eight years old, in fact, my son once told a Justice of the United States Supreme Court that he should "never, ever fly Braniff." Every day when I would bring home the package of airline-related newspaper clippings of the day for evening reading, it would be snapped out of my hands. I was usually the last in my family to read it.

I could always relate to the stories employees told me about how their children would point to the sky and say, "Look, Daddy and Mommy, it's one of our planes." My kids did the same thing.

Chapter 43

The Tactics of Success May Vary, but the Principles Are Constant

As I mentioned elsewhere, one of the things I found intriguing about Texas Roadhouse restaurants is the way that company has used many of the principles on which Southwest Airlines' success was built and applied them in an entirely different industry. Because it is a different industry, some of the applications of those principles do not look familiar.

I already described how surprised I was to learn that most Texas Roadhouse restaurants do not open for lunch. It seemed counterintuitive to me to let an asset as expensive as a restaurant sit idle at lunch, but once I understood the impact on the company's ability to attract top managers and employees, it made perfect sense. It is a great example of how all decisions involve tradeoffs and you have to recognize what is most important.

Another tactic that surprised me involved the assignment of employees to the host area, which is basically the reception desk where customers are greeted. Most casual dining restaurants I had visited seemed to have one person working in the host area, and that person never seemed to be there when I walked in. The person was either seating other customers or answering the telephone to take reservations, give directions, or describe the menu to callers.

At Texas Roadhouse, I learned, seven people are assigned to the host area, each with different but interrelated areas of responsibility. I was shocked. Why do we need seven people? That doesn't seem very efficient.

Fortunately, the people who put together the Texas Roadhouse concept are all very experienced restaurateurs who are not afraid to think outside the box. They know their business inside out, and they know how to make it operate at peak efficiency. If you want to offer legendary food with legendary service at affordable prices, you have to be efficient. And, I was told, it takes seven distinct positions to operate at peak efficiency and deliver superior customer service during rush hours.

But seven positions? What do they all do?

Well, since you asked:

1. The Name Taker greets guests and takes names.
2. The Seater Greeter escorts guests to their tables and seats them.
3. The Updater coordinates the immediate clearing of tables when guests leave and lets everybody in the process know when a table is coming available so that guests will arrive at the table just as it is wiped clean.
4. The To Go Host greets guests either in person or on the phone, takes to go orders, places the order

with the kitchen, packages the order, delivers it to the customer, and concludes the financial transaction.

5. The Call Ahead Host answers the telephones, advises customers of the waiting time, puts customers on the waiting list, and works side by side with the Name Taker to coordinate the efficient use of tables and ensure the accuracy of information given to customers.

6. The Board and Seating Coordinator coordinates seating assignments to ensure proper rotation. This is necessary to ensure that a single server is not assigned multiple new tables of customers at the same time. Having customers sitting around and waiting for a server is not only irritating for customers, but it is bad business. Promptly taking customers' orders is good customer service, and it is an efficient utilization of resources in a business where each table has only a few hours every day to make money.

7. The Large Party Host and Assistant Coordinator handles the often delicate issue of seating large parties. Seating large parties frequently involves difficult decisions concerning the priority of table allocations. Adjacent four-party tables do not usually become available at the same time. Do you seat another party of four or hold the table for a party of six until an adjacent table becomes available?

All of this helped me realize that the restaurant business, like every business, is very complicated and unique. Even though Kent Taylor had told me that Southwest Airlines was his role model when he founded Texas Roadhouse, the application of the fundamental principles on which Southwest was built looked a lot different in the restaurant industry. But if you dug down through the things that looked different, you found that the core values were the same.

For starters, Texas Roadhouse offers its customers the same basic value proposition as Southwest Airlines—low prices, great customer service, and great food. To achieve low costs, assets are used at peak efficiency and there isn't much waste. The company has a strong customer service culture, and all of this produces healthy profits while creating loyal customers.

More important, the company realized the paramount secret to building a culture of customer service—the way you treat employees determines the way they treat customers. Employees enjoy their jobs, and it shows.

People think like owners. When a new restaurant manager is hired, for example, he or she signs a five-year contract to develop a restaurant. This is unusual in the restaurant business, where good managers tend to get moved around a lot. A manager at Texas Roadhouse knows he or she will have five years to develop the business, so there is strong motivation to develop lasting relationships with the community, employees, and customers. Managers receive a base salary that is probably less than they could earn elsewhere. But they also receive a percentage of the net profits of their restaurant. In a successful restaurant, this profit share often equals or exceeds the base salary. In addition, managers receive stock options in Texas Roadhouse. Managers aren't just expected to think like owners; they actually are owners. And it's a fun place to work.

As a consequence, manager positions at Texas Roadhouse restaurants are highly sought after in the industry. Texas Roadhouse doesn't have to recruit new managers; it just selects them from among the best people in the restaurant business. The positions are so coveted that when a new manager is hired, he or she actually pays the company an advance deposit of $25,000.

Employees at Texas Roadhouse not only enjoy their jobs, but they are given the tools to do their jobs and are expected to use their heads to make decisions. Training is extensive. New managers are hired months before a new restaurant is to open, and they receive months of training on Texas Roadhouse procedures. They meet the founder of the company, Kent Taylor; the CEO, G. J. Hart; and the chief operating officer, Steve Ortiz. They learn the passion, history, and culture of the company.

Employees at every level receive careful training before being released to work on their own. For example, taking to go orders may not seem that complicated, but the To Go Host receives three full days of initial training before assuming the job. How do you answer the phone with energy and enthusiasm? What are all the steaks and side items? Describe the appetizers. How do you separate hot items and cold items? What should be done to every steak before it is given to the customer? How do you handle re-cooks? What is good presentation, and why does it matter? If you are missing a menu item, who do you talk to? How do gift cards work?

How do you maintain a positive relationship with guests if something is wrong?

The job is actually more complicated than it looks. It requires employees to use their heads and their personalities. It requires that people know what they are doing. The job has value, and employees who do it are appreciated. Like all the other jobs, it requires people who love their jobs, who understand teamwork, and who want to deliver legendary customer service.

Beneath the differences, the principles of success are still the same. Businesses may differ and tactics may vary, but the fundamental principles of success are pretty much constant.

I think the lesson here is that when leaders in other industries study the legendary success of Southwest Airlines, growing from a startup airline with three airplanes into the largest and most consistently profitable domestic airline in the United States, they should not focus on the specific business tactics that the company employed. Southwest has always had a lot of smart airline people who knew the industry inside out. They knew how to apply certain core values to Southwest's business model. Southwest didn't try to be all things to all people, and all of its tactics were designed to support the specific business model it adopted.

Successful leaders in any industry will need to understand their own business in the same way. They will need to set their own priorities and develop their own practices, which will be unique to their situations. After all, that's what makes free enterprise fun. People can try different things. If something doesn't work, try something else.

But I do think that leaders in any organization will do well if they remember a few of the things I learned from my 25 years of watching the highly motivated, dedicated, and spirited people of Southwest Airlines build the most successful airline in the world. Dedicated employees really do create loyal customers and large profits.

Chapter 44

Be Yourself and Have Some Fun

S hortly after I became CEO of Southwest Airlines, I was invited to speak to a group at The University of Texas at Austin. The presentation was scheduled for 4:30 on a Friday afternoon to accommodate my schedule. When I arrived, I was surprised to see that the room was packed. People were sitting in the aisles and standing in the back of the room. Recalling what we were usually doing by 4:30 on Friday afternoons when I was in school, I quickly concluded that things had certainly changed since I was there.

The audience, consisting mostly of business students, listened with interest to my remarks, even though I didn't talk much about things business students usually expect to hear from corporate CEOs. Mostly I just told them how we owed our success to the resourcefulness and dedication of our employees, how we tried to have some fun while delivering great customer service, and how we tried to practice the Golden Rule.

The students were actually quite receptive to all of this and seemed to soak it in. But these were future leaders of the business world, and they were also interested in developing their own leadership skills. Finally, one student asked the direct question, "What advice would you give me if I want to be a CEO some day?"

I had to confess that I might not be the ideal person to answer that question, since I never aspired to be a CEO, or even to work in the corporate world. In fact, when I was in college, I never even took a course in the business school other than economics, which has since been moved to the college of liberal arts. I was a liberal arts major who just took courses in a wide variety of subjects that I found interesting and stimulating.

That, I concluded, perhaps reflected the best advice I could give. Find something you are passionate about, and follow it wherever it takes you. Do the best you can at whatever you are doing, and opportunities will likely come along. Just be yourself and do something you enjoy. You may or may not end up being a CEO. But if you do your best and enjoy what you are doing, you will probably have a much happier life than if you spend all your time in pursuit of some title or position that you may or may not ever attain. And you will be a lot more fun to be around.

I think that may be pretty good advice for leaders at all levels. Find something you enjoy. Be yourself. Have some fun. Remember that people recognize phonies. They follow leaders they want to follow. They follow leaders who are trustworthy and genuine. Don't try to be something you're not.

People do not like to be used as stepping stones. They want leaders who do the best they can every day, not leaders who spend all their time trying to position themselves for a promotion. They want leaders who help them be the best they can be. Don't try to use people or trick them. Lead them through the example of your words and deeds. Create a culture in which people want to do the right things and want your team to succeed. Make work fun, and people will enjoy their work. Love people, and they will love you back.

Great leaders create great teams through teamwork. Teamwork requires mutual trust and respect throughout the team. It requires employees who love their jobs and want the team to succeed. Great leaders who can produce this kind of atmosphere will have plenty of success and plenty of opportunities.

Finally, don't lose your sense of humor. It helps put some of life's absurdities in their place. Sometimes, if you couldn't laugh at an outrageous situation, you would just go crazy.

And it's okay to take your work seriously, but don't take yourself too seriously. If you stand back and look, you will probably see yourself doing some pretty silly things from time to time. Laughing at yourself every once in a while will help you keep things in perspective. And, hopefully, it will keep you from starting to think you are too damn important.

Chapter 45

It's a Round World

Experience has made me a firm believer in the Round World Theory. The world goes around, and what goes around comes around. We may think that what we did today is done when the sun sets. But it will likely come back around to visit us when the sun rises on some other day.

The way we treat other people largely determines the way they will treat us back. This is one reason why the Golden Rule is not just a good rule of ethics; it is a good rule of business. Treat other people the way you would like them to treat you, and they probably will.

The Round World Theory is demonstrably true in the business world as well. Leaders who are trustworthy will be trusted. Leaders who treat employees with respect will likely be respected. Employees will love their company if it loves them back. And when they love their company and love their jobs, they may create a culture of customer service that will become legendary.

About 18 months after 9/11, I was moved by a newspaper column I ran across from the *Albuquerque*

Tribune. It had been a rough 18 months. Like everybody else in the airline industry, and most Americans, I hadn't found much to enjoy in life during this period. But this column, which was inspired by a random act of compassion by an anonymous employee almost 20 years before, reminded me that everything we do has consequences we may never realize. The column was written by Mr. J. D. Bullington, who I do not know and, to the best of my knowledge, have never met. He wrote, in part:

> Southwest Airlines is now the world's most profitable and most admired airline. Its stock is worth more than all the other big airlines combined and delivers the highest margins in the airline industry— by far.

> Experts say Southwest got there by tempering opportunism with fiscal conservatism, being the leader in increased productivity and having the lowest operating cost per seat mile in the industry. Southwest is the only major carrier to remain profitable in every quarter since 9/11. Its six biggest rivals have laid off more than 70,000 people. [The number ultimately grew even larger.] Southwest has never laid off a soul.

He went on with some stuff about how our president, Colleen Barrett, didn't know how to use e-mail and how I had a beer keg in my office for after-hour employee get-togethers, and then he continued:

You can reference all the management guru jive you want. But I have my own thoughts on why Southwest Airlines is No. 1.

I worked for Ozark Airlines in Denver at Stapleton Airport in the mid-'80s. Ozark owned gates at Stapleton and, because of that, when Southwest flew into Denver, it used Ozark's gates and Ozark employees to load and unload bags.

One night, while I was in the belly of one of Southwest's 737s packing and stacking bags in the rear bin, one of my coworkers handed me a bucket with some tape criss-crossed over the top of it.

"What the hell is this?" I said.

"It's somebody's bag. Pack it."

We laughed at it. We made fun of it. We mocked it.

Somewhere in time, during the infancy of Southwest Airlines, the company developed a culture of customer service that instinctively led a Southwest gate agent on a cold winter night in Denver to show compassion for a poor, struggling passenger, just trying to make his way home. He didn't have luggage. He had a bucket of personal belongings. A bucket! And a Southwest employee took responsibility for it, checked it and carried it down to the ramp, and I packed it.

I may never see a greater, more humbling example of compassionate customer service in my life. ...While other airlines wallow, trying to figure out how to defy the Peter Pan Principle, Southwest flies high because its culture, from the CEO down to the shop steward for the baggage handlers, is all about you, you, you.

This may win the award for most gratuitous column. I don't care. Southwest Airlines deserves it.

The company has the same philosophy since 1971: Get people where they want to go for the lowest fare possible with the best customer service in the industry.

Southwest takes care of people, both employees and customers, and people take care of the company. It's just that simple.

It's just that simple.

Index

ᵁᵁ Wharton School Publishing

In the face of accelerating turbulence and change, business leaders and policy makers need new ways of thinking to sustain performance and growth.

Wharton School Publishing offers a trusted source for stimulating ideas from thought leaders who provide new mental models to address changes in strategy, management, and finance. We seek out authors from diverse disciplines with a profound understanding of change and its implications. We offer books and tools that help executives respond to the challenge of change.

Every book and management tool we publish meets quality standards set by The Wharton School of the University of Pennsylvania. Each title is reviewed by the Wharton School Publishing Editorial Board before being given Wharton's seal of approval. This ensures that Wharton publications are timely, relevant, important, conceptually sound or empirically based, and implementable.

To fit our readers' learning preferences, Wharton publications are available in multiple formats, including books, audio, and electronic.

To find out more about our books and management tools, visit us at whartonsp.com and Wharton's executive education site, exceed.wharton.upenn.edu.